Utopia

By Sharon Bengalrose Healing
and her spirit team

You will be inspired as these pages reveal some of the spirit realm and earth secrets to you. I was thrilled when two new Archangels were revealed to us and an alien race that visited earth many centuries ago.

I know that as you read these pages you will feel various emotions, caused by what has been revealed to you from the spirit world. But you will also know from the essence within you that they are right, because the spirit do not lie. They want the best for mankind and this book guides us to achieve this.

During the process of self-publishing, I was asked if this work was non-fiction or fiction; I have no doubt that this is non-fiction piece. I have lived some of this book as it was written, been inspired as you will be to be that better person. My guides have chosen to word this book and tell their story so that it is for everyday people on earth, everyday people like you and me that will understand its message and spread their love and light.

Enjoy, my friends.

*Fiction is an invented existence,
a world of fantasy and make-believe.*

Non-fiction is truth and the real world.

Which do you live in? Do you dream of a better world?

You can all make this a better, equal, safe world.

Work as one, not against each other.

*Start today; take one-step towards your fantasy world
and it will become your reality.*

Utopia
Copyright © 2015 by Sharon Bengalrose Healing

Published by Bengalrose Healing.
Designed by Sharon Barbour
Author - Sharon's spirit inspiration writing team
Book cover illustration – by Sharon Bengalrose and her spirit team
Editors - Di Reed-copywriter and author. Chris Barbour - husband and soul
mate. Rebecca Fowler-aquaintence.

Welcome, my friends

Love and blessings

Utopia is heaven, heaven is Utopia, beauty, paradise and pure love, but these are just words, your soul holds the known beauty of heaven my friends. Your home will always be our realm, but when you return to us, you will always carry a small part of your lives' you choose to live on planets and other realms back to us. The essence of that life form and their language will always be a part of you. Every life you choose to live is part of your learning path and will always hold new inspirations for your soul, bringing them back home. The path you will always aim to tread while in that life is for positivity, inspiration and wisdom so you can trigger the light bulb moment of finding love and light and spirit to guide you.

Welcome, my friends

My world – with age-old wisdom from the spirit realm.

I will show you how to ensure the future of mankind by working with the spirit realm, and how to build a world of love and enlightenment.

Wisdom derives from ancient worlds from bygone ages across the void of space and time. My world Utopia is timeless and full of wisdom. Who am I? I am Harold and come from the realm of Utopia. I have spent time amongst you and my life on earth was as a Benedictine monk in the medieval ages. I was a philosopher in my lifetime on earth; I also guided others to record your history, stories and beliefs in the beautiful manuscripts you admire today from those times.

At the moment, one of my chosen roles is a lifetime guide to Sharon; I am an overseer in her spirit family and have been working with her inspiration-writing path. At first, Sharon did not understand why she was chosen but now, she does not question why; she knows she is a channel for the power source like many others of mankind are, and she has put her trust in her guidance team and me. We managed to trigger this in her when she started trance mediumship, a lovely energy level for us to connect with mankind. We can use this trance state to talk to you, mind to mind, and give guidance to you.

As you read this book, you will question the facts. Are they true? Believe me, all the books from the light workers about angels and the spirit realm and how we work with you are true. We now feel mankind should know more about our realm. There will always be those amongst you who will question any written text, especially if it contradicts your existing beliefs and adds more questions to the human mind and existence. But that is your ego; just ask: Can I trust this new knowledge? My friends, you will know the answer in your hearts and inner beings.

As well as enlightening you about us, we have included a couple of chapters in the book that answer questions from you, and tell your stories about glimpses into Utopia. I asked for these to be sourced for me via your modern technology communication online sources and friends. We requested questions that challenge you and your existence, about the universe and your life's path. We know the questions will resonate with many of you, and you will draw comfort and guidance from the answers. Other chapters are full of small examples from earth's legends and stories. Remember my friends, most of these stories and legends will stem from real events and facts from hundreds or thousands of years ago. Mankind would have written these with their understanding and language of that time. Over time, some of them have been rewritten or added to; it is up to you to investigate, debate, tune in and use your intuition to know what is correct. I look forward to seeing your reactions as you read these chapters, as I will be sitting beside you on this journey.

We are working hard with all mediums, healers, and those of you on a spiritual path, which we call light workers, to spread our messages of love and light. We do this through your spirit circles, spirit churches, holistic healers and trance groups. We also work with you all from your birth, steering you on the path of enlightenment to spread our love. This lies within you all like a light bulb waiting to be switched on. Once this happens, and you see the love and light, then we rejoice, for this is the start of your journey of learning and the fun of living in love and light. I get very excited at these moments in mankind's existence!

As mankind has developed, we have been looking at ways to work with you to improve how we can communicate. I have to admit I was unsure of the speed at which mankind had developed technology and how it has effected your face-to-face communication skills; I felt it had taken some of your core humanity away from you. But I now realise how this technology can quickly spread our messages of love and light to your modern world, as well as verbal face-to-face contact. We have found that trying to connect with you around your world of technology is harder because of the hidden energy waves, but we are adapting to improve this.

This book has been written so you can start to understand the stories of your world, to ignite your interest in mankind, and start your journey of learning and discovering yourself, exploring your world to ensure a better future for mankind. Start with the ancient history marks left on old civilisations walls, and the unanswered questions mankind has about your own mortality. I have just given you from your existing pot of earth knowledge, reminders of what already exists on your earth – and there is so much more to discover. Your challenge is to educate yourselves, read, discuss your thoughts with like-minded people, and spread our messages out to your fellow mankind. As a great man Mahatma Gandhi of your time said:

"We must be the change we wish to see in the world".

Think of this as you read these pages.

I have also added inspirational quotes in a chapter at the end of the book, I hope they inspire you; and please use them to inspire others around you. We ask you to communicate our words to your world. We know if you are now reading this book it is part of your life's path to do so.

As I explain to you about my realm Utopia, I can only use the words you know and try to explain as best I can by using language you will recognise; your imaginations will do the rest.

Spark of life

A spark, a light in the dark

A glimpse of hope

The light casts a shadow

The shadow stretches before you

Always beside you

You are the light

We are the shadow

Even in the dark

Our shadow is with you

Light your spark to see us

Hear us and feel us

Sparkle and shine bright

Chapter 1

Who are we?

We would like to take you back to a time, long, long ago in your distance past, when your world was young, a baby in the growing universe. She was a pure planet – her energy vibrated across the stars to our realm and others – your planet Earth called to us.

We search for planets that can hold what you know as life forms. At the moment we are in close contact with over a 1000 fold of planets, realms or dimensions. We are also observing other realms for possible contact. We search for entities that can hold our pure spirit inside them and develop, so we can gain knowledge from you for our self-growth.

We are your soul – a fact that can be mind-blowing for some. Your body is our shell and although you have your own individual essence that makes you human, combined with our spirit you are so much more, because you have true, pure love in your inner being from birth. Your spirit, or soul as you like to say, is here on earth to develop and learn; part of your spirit remains in our realm, interacting with you on earth, and the rest of us here, the part of you that is your higher self. Think of us as pure energy souls that are a spark of the divine light having a physical experience. We all exist in what I can best describe to you a conscious beautiful energy hologram and we all create our own reality with in it.

We have been part of your lives for thousands of years, waiting for you to develop and gain knowledge. Only when we can learn from a planet or realm as we grow and develop, can we become part of you. Even going back all those years when mankind was more primitive, we learned from your basic life styles and watched how you grew and developed. It is around

10,000 years ago when you had a growth in development and your world populations started to grow that we really started to learn with you, and could become more and more a part of your existence.

We have watched mother earth for a very long time with the help of Utopians that are discoverers, researchers who monitor planets, other realms and dimensions for life forms. We do not intervene too much in your progress; we like you all to have free will. When we blend with a life form, your life's path is born into your essence; we wait for you to discover the light and the love we shower down on you, before we can really help. This is how you, and the other life forms we are involved with, grow stronger, and we learn from blending with them.

The universe is made of different dimensions, layers and levels of energy. What mankind has seen of the universe so far is just the tipping point of unimaginable things. Our realm sits in a dimension within the vast universe make-up. We have named our realm Utopia for you to understand us more as in your languages it means heaven, paradise, bliss and an imagined place or state of things in which everything is perfect. Well, Utopia (heaven) is very real and to explain our realm's beauty, it is made up of pure love, a place with no sadness, grief or heartache; we only know joy and thrive from the knowledge and wisdom we learn from you all and each other.

Your imaginations over the centuries have written stories of our realm as we allowed you to see glimpses into it, but there have been other influences that you will discover in this book. Throughout mankind's development, different civilisations and religions have emerged - this is mankind's interpretation of your alien soul and inner power that you have struggled to explain. On the occasions we have shown ourselves we are seen as miracles, and mankind has been given hope in times of despair. We often hear your voices of despair; you have free will and yet you choose to self-destruct often, as your history timelines show us. We do not intervene very often on planets' courses in hope that you will learn from these events. Before you come to earth, your main goal is to bring enlightenment to mankind – and oh boy, what a challenge this is for you! When one of you sees the light and asks for help, then we can step in and help you on your journey. Until then we watch you travel your life's path, nudging you where we can, giving signs to follow and bringing you safely home when it is your time to return to us.

Our vision
is your vision,
live it,
breath it,
we will be in it.

The overseers of Utopia

On earth, you have laws that help you run your countries and societies, which give you structure and guidance. Our realm works in levels of hierarchy, and in common with all civilisations, we have a basic order to follow and guide us.

We have 64 ascension development levels of progression throughout the realm. As we grow in knowledge and wisdom, our powers get stronger. By powers, I mean our inner being gaining strength and all-understanding knowledge of the universe. At each level we reach, we can travel further out in the universe, be assigned more entities to look after, and are given more high-level responsibilities. Some of us of pure spirit that have not walked amongst entities will become guardian angels and Archangels, as you know them. They have gained all our knowledge and wisdom from our source of pure love. Their essence stays pure, which makes them powerful as they ascend the levels. The Utopians that choose to interact with entities absorb a different energy that mixes with their own; this affects our pureness of energy, which is why Arch and Guardian angels do not blend with other life forms. They remain the pure Utopian love source energy needed to carry out their powerful all-knowing role within Utopia.

I'd like to explain that the high ruler, or source of all love, is a being of Love – a pure, all-knowing spirit source, that some of you name 'God' or 'Forever divine loving spirit'. This is the energy source that gives us Utopians life. It is forever lasting, all-knowing and seeing, and sources its strength from love, knowledge and wisdom. All Utopians are born from this source of pure love.

Our next main levels are our overseers, equivalent to the kings, queens and presidents of your world. The best way to explain the role of the overseers is as managers of the realm, planning and making sure all is well within. To reach this stage of development, the Utopians who hold these positions have gone through many of our ascension levels, as far as 55, to obtain the experience, foresight and wisdom required of them.

Humans look up to their leaders; not all are admired by mankind, but Utopians are all interconnected and work as one, respecting each other no matter in what level of the realm we sit, trusting, knowing and guiding so we are all working for the greater good of Utopia. But we are free thinking individuals too. I know that this is a lot for you to take in. Our overseers guide and advise us, interacting at all levels to make sure the best is achieved for the greater good of all.

Angels

Then we have our Archangels – filled with the all-knowing, purest of love. These high-ranking Utopians hang out in the highest levels of our ascension levels. We have already worked alongside some of your light workers to explain about the Archangels assigned to earth, giving them names and powers.

There are so many others you are unaware of as yet; they work within our realm, other dimensions and planets.

I would like to introduce you to an Archangel called Tyron, who oversees the progressions of Utopians on their development journey through the ascension levels. Archangel Tyron has gained so much wisdom and knowledge; he is a great overseer of us in Utopia on our life paths. He has other archangels helping him and they learn from him. He has not had much to do with mankind, but he knows all we have gained from you. He has a very philosophical way of looking at things; his main strength to us is as an advisor, and he is a great planner. We would portray him to you with penetrating eyes and you would be lost in the pools of wisdom they hold. His face would be more aged with an all-knowing angelic glow.

Archangel Shanderal will also be new to you, and to you she will have a more feminine energy. She oversees our realms that are equivalent to your nature. As our nature and creatures die back the energy is absorbed back in to our realm; she oversees the flow of this and the distribution of their energy back to the source; this is done with great love as all living things have feelings. Imagine on your earth as you walk through a field, you run your hands through the grass and pull off the tops; every one of those plants will feel this and it will affect their energy flow and vibrate through them. As your plants die back in the winter seasons, Mother Nature absorbs their energy. Our Love source absorbs our nature's energy, and Shanderal oversees this process. To you, Shanderal would have more of a pixie fairy look, beautiful and flowing, delicate and light of heart, pouring her love over Utopia, protecting all our nature. She also has a small work crew of angels, helping her extend her knowledge out to them.

Overseeing all of these Angels in Utopia is Ultorium, the highest ranking of all the angels. If mankind were to portray him, he would have a large shield for protection and a lantern for light leading the way. His strength is all-knowing power and wisdom, and he inspires all Utopia by what he has become. His power of great goodness is from time beyond your imagination. He is not destined to come among men with support and guidance as, for example, Archangel Michael does. He is one of many who sits by the great power source, the divine light, God.

Next are the beautiful Guardian Angels. Guardian Angels are at a younger stage of their development; they have to earn their wings – if you don't mind the earth pun. As their name suggests, they guard us while we are with you on your life's journey on earth. You are all assigned your own Guardian Angel, who will be with you for your whole earth life. Others will be assigned to you as needed as you develop on your life's path. The guardian angels can be assigned more than one entity to oversee, depending on their stage of development.

Throughout your history, Mankind has portrayed our Archangels and Guardian Angels with wings in paintings – this is because our energy form leaves a flow of shimmering light behind us as we move and to the humankind eye, it can resemble wings. You portray us in this form, so we show ourselves like this so you feel comfortable and will recognise us at the times we choose to reveal ourselves to you.

You have books that already exist, revealing some of this knowledge on earth and how the Archangels can help you; we will let you explore these books yourselves.

Turn Dark into light

If you are feeling your days are dark
Pause…
Light a candle and make a wish
Listen…
We are all around you to give you strength
Feel…
Ask for a sign from us to be near
See…
It might be an angel feather
Touch…
We will touch your heart and inspire you
You…
You are loved and precious to us
Light…
Light your candle and shine into your world
Love…
Love is all around you, love yourself.

Spirit families

Within Utopia, there are groups of Spirits at various levels of development – each group is like a large happy family. We have Spirit family overseers; they oversee these family spirit groups and their development. They are made up of teachers, healers, knowledge searchers and support networkers; they nurture, guide and help develop us, both in Utopia and when we are amongst you.

The Spirit families are made up from very young Utopian energies to the higher-level energies that are assigned to the groups overseeing them. We do not have parents, brothers and sisters as you do on earth. But we are in large family support network groups, and you would recognise them as soul groups in your understanding.

As we have explained, we are a realm world in a dimension level. Utopia is a realm of great never-ending beauty. It is not a round planet like earth and other planets. When you return home to us and your soul group you will understand this miracle of its existence. There is no poverty or hate, just love, caring, guiding and nurturing of each other, living in pure love existence.

Re-birth in Utopia

Do we experience birth and death? Yes! Birth is joy but our death is joy too. We do not know time; as your many centuries pass we still remain young in our realm, but when we do reach that stage to pass over we go to our love source and we give our energy and life force source to new spirits and our energy is reborn. Our essence then exists in other Utopians as your humankind genes do when you create a new life. Our energy forms age, as do all other life forms. The best way to explain it is to imagine we are car batteries that recharge and eventually, the batteries wear out. We know when we are ready, and our ageless wisdom and knowledge is passed on in our gifts of life to our realm, and we live on in others. We do this gladly as it is our natural progression for us - old becoming new, our essence living on in new spirits, building old age wisdom, forever developing and learning. Our essence and all we have learnt will be part of them, pure from time beyond.

Each young Utopian has the support of our love energy source and some inner knowledge to draw on as they begin their spiritual journey. When they join their spirit family, there are various levels of development and nurturing they will be guided through. The families' love and spiritual development help the young Utopians grow. They have the family overseers and Archangels to help guide each family group. Some of the family members will remain working in the realm and others will choose to go to a planet or another realm for further development.

We have form; we are conscious beings, each with our own energy footprint, unique to each individual. You would say we have our own personalities. The same as mankind, we grow, develop and learn, and this helps us be who we are as individuals. We have glowing, beautiful energy and auras, but no gender. I say no gender, but we have discovered that our energies can seem more feminine or masculine to you depending on your individual essences. For example, a female human can be more masculine and a man more feminine than others, which can affect how you sense and see our energy when we blend into your energy fields.

We do not need air like you do; our energy source is our equivalent of your air. We do shed extra energy as you do skin cells; when this happens, the realm's source gathers it up and it is recycled back into the great source of pure light and love. The appearance of our realm is like your brightest sunny day; I think if you popped into our world in your human form now, as you read this, you would need some of your very powerful sunglasses!

As we develop and grow in Utopia we change within our being. Each time we blend with humans, and other entities, we absorb some of your pure uniqueness; as we return to our realm, this becomes part of our energy footprint and Utopia. As we work with all species, we change and develop all the time for the greater good.

Utopia's palaces

The Utopian families dwell amongst exquisite beauty. We do not have individual house structures to live in like you do on earth, we have family dwellings – areas where we meet and recharge our-self with our life source energy. Imagine your most beautiful palaces, cathedrals that glitter like diamonds or cool marble, and then you can start to imagine what our world structures are like. Take the best of your world and multiply it a thousand-fold.

Our source of love and light has created beautiful recreational areas and beautiful creatures as you have never seen, colours and vibrancy as never imagined; Utopia has to be seen to be believed. The noise of our world is like a tune in perfect key, the sound of harmonious tranquillity.

The overall look of Utopia has a shimmering golden glow, the feel of your rising sun on a summer's day. There are gentle shifting colours in the realm. Our skies are shifting changing colours; where we dwell is lush with plants as you would understand them and shades of colours unseen by the human eye. The Utopian equivalent of your plant life is like looking at flowers, giant to your eyes, that shimmer and sparkle, all-moving with the energy flow of our realm. They don't have roots, they are there, being, part of the energy stream. As they move you can see their energy trail left behind, a bit like looking at one of your firework sparklers when you move it in your air at night.

We only have one season, like one of your perfect summer's days. Our realm is created by our divine source energy. When a life ends in our creatures and our nearest form to your plants, its energy is recycled back to the divine source, forever circulating; think of it as re-cycling.

The gentle creatures that live among us in the realm are as loving and caring to the Utopians as we are to them. They exist as we do from the pure love energy sources, but their life span is less than spirit Utopians. They are not our pets; they exist alongside us. We also have areas of flowing energy in the realm. To you, this would be like looking at your water falls, falling into pools, but golden energy sparkling, jumping and shimmering. We exist, moving and being; I suppose floating would be the nearest word I can find to explain this, flowing along on what you would think of as a gentle breeze. The beauty of each world and realm we visit is reflected in ours, with the knowledge and creatures we see and learn about.

In our recreational time in Utopia we love to create music and express the beauty of our world through what you would think of as dance and arts. I use these words so you can try to understand us; we have similar passions, and although what we have is so different from every individual planet and realm we link with, that is what we love. As well as learning, we like time for what you would call hobbies and pleasure in our existence, as we learn from this also.

As we explore new planets and entities, we discover so much that then helps with our creativity in our realm. We live a relaxed existence, the stress and worries of the world you experience we do not have in our divine existence. But please remember - all the worlds and realms we visit are unique and beautiful in their own ways. Our realm has become what it is from all we have learned and the wisdom we have developed from our journeys.

We do not experience day and night as you do. While you recharge your energy overnight, we recharge during rest periods, when we meet up with our family groups and connect with the pure love source. We have time, but not as you do; your lifetime on earth is just a fraction of your time existence in Utopia. Every life form we come across in the realms and worlds we visit, has a different time frame, making it very interesting for us to learn from.

Time is the essence of your existence;
look beyond time to find your true self.

The way Utopians communicate

We communicate amongst ourselves by telepathic language and also can be recorded by us in our own unique way. But we mainly communicate by our own spirit energy source, which is the equivalent of your mind (brain). We hear, see and have the ability to block out all our busy thoughts, apart from other Utopians or beings, from whom we need to communicate and receive thoughts. As we develop and progress on our journeys, gaining higher ascension within our realm, our skill for communication grows greater and we develop an all-knowing awareness, but we have to work to develop these skills. Our psychic abilities are well beyond your development, but you are all capable of much more. We are also able to transport ourselves physically with our thoughts. We do not need any vehicle transport as you do, as we can what you call teleport round our realm. We can also do this out to other worlds and dimensions, but this is a privilege that we earn as we reach higher levels in our development.

Those of you that have been attuned through your spirit and healing work to come closer to our frequency, can hear us and feel us. How do you think this book was written? I sent the thoughts to the writer telepathically, mind to mind, and she received them, interpreting them as best she could, then together, we went over the content a few times, editing until we were happy.

Every entity we choose to be with has a group of spirits from our realm that will be with you throughout your life. You have at least three guardian angels that stay with you all the time. You also have a team of spirit guides. Guides are spirits that have lived amongst you on earth and understand humankind ways, as well as having experienced them. During your life, some of these guides will leave you and new ones will come in. This will be at key times on your life's path, for example: Mother or fatherhood, education, health and enlightenment. I like to call them your team, and they are waiting for you to become aware of their existence and to communicate with them. My friends, when this spark of enlightenment happens we are overjoyed.

Another way we can attune to your mother earth is through her crystals. This has been a way for us to help connect with you over the centuries, through holistic healing times up to modern day. Mother Earth's crystals and gemstones have been valued for thousands of years for their healing and spiritual properties. Formed within the layers of the Earth, each crystal has its own unique colour, vibration and purpose. The crystals can harness energy, which we use to strengthen our links to you. I would like to highlight an old human legend about the thirteen human skull crystals from many hundreds of years ago, believed to be a power source for a highly developed race. When the society collapsed, the skulls were spread around the world for safekeeping. Over time, some of them have been taken in by collectors and the chosen protectors of your relics, but some of mankind have tried to say that the story is fake, and mankind has also created fake skulls.

You have to think: were these crystal skulls a way for them to communicate with their higher selves, knowledge and other dimensions, or were they just a power symbol of a religious belief system you know nothing about? Now look at your modern day technology. A company in Japan showed mankind its ability to encode data onto "quartz glass". Data is etched into the material and it is thought that it should last 100 million years. I say to you, my friends, if modern man can make this discovery then imagine what could be stored in ancient crystal material left by highly intelligent races from other worlds, including us. You just need to tap into it to receive these messages.

The way mankind communicates with each other has made a massive technological leap in the last 100 years, from the first postage letter to millions of emails a day, from smoke signals to mobile phones, paper books to books being read on computers and E-books. With the tap of a button you have access to vast knowledge, images, news and life around your world. This is just the tip of the iceberg for you all, my friends, but your main communication since mankind came to earth is verbal. Also try using your senses to understand how another feels - one way is by looking deep into humankind eyes, feel what they are feeling, and what they are communicating to you.

As mankind leaps forward with all this technology, through-out this fast development you are losing your verbal communication skills, and a lot of your young people in the modern world have trouble socialising and communicating with others. You must make sure these skills are not completely lost, because social interaction is very important for the future of mankind.

Great minds and alien intervention have helped you get to the point you are today. What mankind keeps suppressed is a large part of their brain; your telepathic communication skills sit within you all, you just need to switch it on. If you could tap into this and go up to a higher vibration, you would all become aware of a lot more of what is around you. You would become aware of other dimensions, tapping into great universal knowledge and wisdom. Your world would accelerate into a high level society, all-working as one, for the greater good of YOU and mother earth. You would be enlightened and your individual intelligence would be awesome. How your world would change!

For years, your scientists have been working with the mind and telepathic breakthroughs that have been made, but kept suppressed from you. Also, some of the aliens that have made contact communicate this way with the secret parts of your governments. The leaders of your world choose not to share the leaps forward they have found; the fear is greed, and how to keep a grip on society. If mankind could unlock their minds, the universe would be yours for the exploring.

Individually, you can explore your minds. Meditation helps rest your mind, clearing it so you can tune into us. Call us to you; your guides are waiting for you to ask. If you can tune into us, you can tune into each other, which is food for thought. Your ascension would be higher; you would be more knowing in your existence, of yourself and all around you. At that higher accession level of mankind, you would move beyond wars, you would make your countries equal, all of mankind would live as one, helping each other to achieve your full potential. This is not a dream, and will happen over time. This is mankind's hope, what you are all striving towards, and what we all know you want to achieve. I would like to give one example for you of how we can work with you all – a man who lived over 50 years ago called Edgar Cayce. Through meditation, he had the ability to connect with us and the knowledge pot of the universe. He was an amazing ambassador for our realm and his life and foundation for research enlightenment has carried on to this time. Research Edgar, my friends, and learn from him.

I would like at this stage to explain to you about the third (3D), fourth (4D) and fifth (5D) dimensions. I am sure you have heard of these. Mankind lives in the third dimension at the moment; this is a busy, chattering dimension with fear and feelings of powerlessness and loss in the world you live in. You feel you want to do more for your world but you are swimming against a heavy current, living in hope the tide will change. The third dimension has now served its purpose, with mankind coming to the point where you can now lift yourselves out of it.

When I talk of meditation, and connecting with your suppressed powers and reaching enlightenment, this is so you can raise your vibrations and awareness to what we call the fifth dimension levels.

The fourth dimension is what I call the middle ground, the stepping-stone to the fifth. The fourth dimension is smoother flowing with ease, offers possibility and capability, more hope to mankind. You are already starting to work in this dimension with the shift since your year 2000. Since around 2012 the shift has accelerated and there is notable changes in mankind and their attitude to changing spiritually. The more of you that lift your vibration the more of you will be transported to the fourth dimension way of thinking and being. Your earth will become more enlightened and the shift will really be moving along at a fast pace.

The fifth dimension exists in a permanent state of peace, bliss, love and joy and in it, you may also begin to automatically feel love for everyone. No more negative thoughts will stream into the mind of a being who has reached fifth dimension consciousness. Your mind is quieter, allowing for telepathic skills; you will be without the constant chatter that flows into the third dimension mind. While in this wonderful fifth dimension, you can also connect to the universe knowledge pot. You've probably guessed by now in which dimension level Utopia exists. Mankind can exist at this level on earth in your human form, if you lose your layers of doubt and fear. There is a lot of information in your earth's knowledge about this subject, which will fascinate you. The veil is being lifted off Mother earth so you can shift into the higher dimensions, which is what a lot of you tuned into spirit are now feeling. We are very busy working behind the scenes to help take mankind into this level of ascension.

When we say a shift is occurring, the layers between the realms are very thin at the moment, and this allows us to channel 5D energy to your 3D level to help you along. Being the middle platform, the fourth (4D) dimension is there to help you to take the next leap of faith and TRUST.

Our relationship with Earth

Please remember that we decided a long time ago to give all our planets and realms we visit and live among free will – this is vital to our relationship with you all. Those of you who have been enlightened will know you have a team of guides and angels that work with you every day. We will listen and place guidance and signs in your head and around you. But you make the ultimate decision whether or not to follow them. Everything we do is for your greater good, so you can develop and learn to your full potential. Giving you free will sets the challenge amongst you to make you stronger, and defines who you are as a person. The knowing to come back home is then in your spirit, and on your return we all gain knowledge from what you have learnt. If in this lifetime you have not learned all the knowledge you wished to gain, you may choose to come back into another life to do so.

Your free will has caused a lot of sadness over thousands of years as mankind fight each other in wars. Your world is full of armies and weapons, and some of your societies suppress their people if they do not have their leaders' beliefs. We have no need for armies, we have no wars, we do not harm others in our world or other worlds; it is truly as you have heard – all love and forgiveness. If we took your human free will away, you would all live in harmony as we wish you to, because you would follow your inner light and us. This is the challenge for each one of you: all your societies can live in free will and see the light and make their own decisions for the greater good for all, turning your world into a free thinking planet existing in the fifth dimension way of being.

I hear some of you ask, *"Why don't you just come down here and make earth the happy place you want it to be?"* Because you are here to learn, my friends, and learning is never an easy path for any of us. There are always challenges; humans just need to see the light, ask, develop and learn and your earth world will become more like ours. It won't ever be the same, as all realms and worlds are unique, but earth could be a beautiful Utopia in its own right.

You will all have had times on your life's path when, if you sense you are in danger or a dark negative mind place, your inner being (soul) will cry out to your higher self for help; when this happens, we will help and support you from Utopia. When you start to see the light on your path, you will recognise these past events and know we have guided and been with you through them.

We are building our relationship more and more with mankind; one of the many ways is through light workers. We have gathered vast knowledge from lives spent on earth for our realm. We can of course gain this existing knowledge without coming to Earth, but there is nothing better than each one of us experiencing first-hand what we wish to learn. This ingrains it into our spirit and makes us better teachers. This is also what mankind should do – you cannot discuss a topic and pass judgement unless you have lived and experienced it, but many of you think you can. Your world is and has been full of philosophers, political groups debating mankind subjects over time, your free will making judgements. But you can only truly judge if you are there first-hand and experience that moment in time and space. Your light workers experience us as spirits first-hand, and they have become the advocates for our realm.

I should also mention that Utopians have free will too. But we do not judge anything or give an opinion unless we have experienced it. We can absorb so much knowledge, then we select what we would like to experience, then the place where we can go to do it – i.e. earth – and make a life plan to achieve this. On reflection, if we have not learnt the lesson fully as we planned, we can choose to go back and try again on earth or another realm or world, or we might select another subject to learn, or take on a new role in Utopia.

Chapter 2

Questions our spirit world is often asked

From the moment we are created in Utopia, we are loved and start on a spiritual path of growth and enlightenment, gaining all knowledge and wisdom of the ages past and future. In my realm, I join with my spirit family for the course of my spirit journey; together, we form a nurturing support structure on our learning journey in Utopia. As part of our development, some of us will go to other planets or realms together and be with each other while on our journeys of learning; we really enjoy this and find it exciting to do.

As humans develop on your earth's journey you become more aware of unusual feelings, and things start to spark off in your minds and inner being about your existence. You might think, *"Have I been here before?"*, or might use the expression, *"I have found my soul mate."* This is because you have recognised a member of your family from the spirit world and are linked on this life's path. A soul mate is someone who knows you better than yourself; your bond will never be broken and your souls will always be linked. Or you may think, *"I feel like I have known you before."* Yes you have; listen to your first thoughts – this is your intuition, it is a gift from us and it is always right.

These unexplained feelings you get throughout your life's journey on earth make you question your existence, which is what you should be doing. This is part of the learning, knowledge and wisdom you will gain on your life's journey.

We have gathered some questions from you that you wished to ask us; they are unedited and we have answered them to help guide you on your life's path. You can share these answers with your fellow mankind, as you all ask the same questions across your world.

We do hear your thoughts and questions, for example: *"What happens when our animals pass over?"* As our realm has developed, all animals we care for in our lives on various planets come and join us; they are spirit from our lowest levels, starting on their development. We hear you sometimes say, *"I'll come back as a dog in my next life!"* Well, you have probably already been one. Food for thought!

We hear you ask: *"How on earth can all this be real and planned? Would it not take great organization?"* You will never fully understand us until you return home to us, so don't even try. Trust in us, you do have a plan to follow and a life's purpose. As you are born, you lose all knowledge of this in your human form, but your higher self, still in our Utopia, knows, as do your guides and angels. Part of your journey is to recognise your path, see the signs and develop enlightenment of your soul on earth, so when you return home to us, you have grown in spirit and wisdom.

It is natural for you to ask questions, as humans are naturally curious. So I know you will enjoy these questions from some of your fellow mankind and the answers from our realm.

As we wrap our arms around you
we lift your pain away

Your questions are answered, my friends

Sam - Am I on the right path?

This question is the right question to ask your self regularly. It is important to take a look at yourself and where you are on your life's journey. If you are questioning it, then there are changes that need to be made. Sit back and look at yourself and ask: *"Are you happy?"* What areas of your life are you not happy with? What can YOU do to change this? When you have your answers, you then need to look inside yourself to find the strength to change things for the better. We are here to listen and guide you to your right path.

Carl - How hard is it to make contact with our physical world and can any spirit do it? Also I'd be interested to know about the process of reincarnation, is there a minimum time that has to pass before this can happen?

This is a powerful question, thank you my friend.

On the first part of the question: The more experienced spirit will easily be able to make contact, the less experienced spirit might need some support from other Utopians to help them. Also, the energy vibration of each human contact needs to be right before we try to connect. The universe is a mass of energy running on different frequencies. In Utopia, we are on a higher vibration energy level; mankind runs on a lower energy vibration. Some of you are born with a more natural ability from birth to connect with us, but as you grow, it is suppressed if it is not nurtured. Others develop this ability and become healers and mediums in your world; they learn to raise this energy vibration up to us, and we have learned to drop ours so the two can meet. When this happens we can pass on messages and energy healing. We get very excited at this, as our love is allowed to shine into your world. Imagine what a different world you would all live in if you developed this ability. When a Utopian wants to connect to someone on earth for the first time, it will be a weaker link as they have to learn to blend with human energy, but your saying 'practice makes perfect' is true.

The second part of the question: We do quite often choose to come back to a planet or realm we have been to before. The main reason for this would be to extend our knowledge of this planet and revisit some lessons not yet learnt on previous visits. We would not come straight back, as when we go home to Utopia we need time to adjust to our world, and reflect on knowledge and lessons learned. As for time scale – in your world it could be within a few years we return to incarnate, or centuries; it would not be days. But remember, my friend, we might choose to reincarnate on another planet or realm.

Sue - In all honesty, my question would be: "how much longer do I have to wait?

I have mixed feelings about this question. I am pleased this lady knows she's coming home, but saddened she wants to leave your world so quickly. She especially needs help and guidance to find her life's purpose and peace with you all. As I send these thoughts, I am sending healing to her and wishing her great happiness.

Bruce - I would ask: "Are we in for any surprises, such as will there be a great difference from that which we are taught about spirit world, and the reality when we get there?"

Yes, there will be a great difference from the sense of the appearance of our realm, the beauty, love and pure spirit, which you can only imagine. If you are lucky, earth angels will have touched you while you are on earth, and you will have had a small taste of the love you will experience when you return home.

The more enlightened your life on earth, the more it will help you adapt easily when you get back home to Utopia, as it won't be such a shock when you hit the love and light energy here. But if you lead a life of sadness, in a dark place, then when you return home the pure love is more of a shock. We very gently ease you back to your old Utopian self; the parts of your earth life that have darkened your spirit are taken away, but only after you have evaluated the lessons you have learned, and passed on the knowledge you have gained for the rest of us to learn.

As to teachings about the Spirit world, my friend, you will find true teachings if you join a spirit church; they will embrace this for you, but there is yet so much more mankind has to receive from us for you to learn. We are patiently trying to feed it to you; this book is an example of that. One of the areas we are developing is teaching you and your children about spiritualism and clearing their minds to raise their energy and vibration.

Give over your most inner personal thoughts to us;
we are listening and here to guide you.
Feel our love all around you.

Emily – "Do you choose to stay to communicate with the earthly plane, or get ready to be reincarnated? Can you do both?"

First part of the question: I like this question, as we love to communicate with you and pass on healing messages and guidance to help you on your journey's path. We do choose to communicate, as those loved ones we have left behind go though questions about their own mortality and what more is there. We guide you to books and knowledge to help you try to understand the next stage of your journey back home. We work though mediums and healers to help you with the answers you seek. Sadly though, unless you have become more aware yourself or of the light workers and their messages, you block our voices and guidance.

The second part of the question: We do quite often choose to return to a planet or realm we have already been to before we reincarnate. As we have a higher self back in our realm, yes we can communicate with our earth past life loved ones as well as being incarnated. Although we have an overseer that helps with all this, we might not always be available to communicate – that has to be planned.

Andrew - Are you with your loved ones?

Understandably, this question is one of the most asked questions by mankind when they grieve, and it is a delight to be able to answer it for you. When you come to earth, your life is planned so that some members of your spirit family come down to earth to be part of your life, and some stay behind in Utopia to work as guides with you.

As you will all return home at different times, it is natural for you to wonder if you will see your loved ones again. When your time of passing over arrives, we have your lifetime guide and at least a couple of familiar spirit family members to bring you safely home to us and help with the transition.

Those of you who have seen the light and trust in what you believe will find parting from your loved ones easier at the time of loss, as you know they come home safe to meet up again at your passing over. After losing a loved one, the ones left behind on earth will always miss their physical presence and personalities – it is natural for you to feel this. You do heal with time; please know, my friends that you will all be together again someday.

Liz - Can communication be stronger if we accept spirit more in our lives?

Yes! Communication will be stronger if you are more open to spirit, as it lifts your vibration and awareness. Most of you walk around blocking us out, but if you let your shutters down and open up more, we can connect better with you.

My advice would be to go to a spiritual church or centre so this connection can be controlled, and you feel safe and understand the experiences you will have. You will find mediation is a great way to start to your spiritual journey to help you connect to us.

Angie - Do our loved ones in spirit see all we do?

When you come back home to our realm, you can look in on your loved ones in that lifetime and observe them from our realm when you choose, as others in Utopia can see how you are doing in your life's journey and your interactions with others. Your guides and angels assigned to you will be with you all the time observing, trying to guide and help you.

Charlie - Who is the first person to greet you when you pass to the spirit world?

You are guided back by your lifetime guardian angel and a couple of your chosen spirit family. We don't overpower you with the whole of your family meeting you, we gradually let you adapt and you gently blend back in. You are given as long as you need and the time of adjustment you need will depend on what your life was on earth and what you learned from it.

Michelle - I have lots of questions but I suppose I would first ask: "What is the biggest lesson we can learn in this life to help us move forward, love, forgiveness, acceptance, something else?"

When you choose to live on a planet or realm, every single one of you has done so to extend your knowledge and grow spiritually. Love, forgiveness and acceptance are some of the reasons; how you interact with each other, or learn to give unselfishly to aid others, are other reasons. But all your life plans will have good, loving intentions. As this memory is wiped from you as you come down to earth, you have your inner essence, which needs to be tapped into; the challenge is to find the pure love light path and your purpose. Some of you do not achieve all the goals of your life plan, but there will be other lessons learned we had not thought of at the time of making your plan; whether good or bad lessons, we absorb them and place them in our knowledge pot for future learning.

Megan - Why show yourself to some but not others?

Following on from the previous question, some of you in your life plan will have allowed for us to show ourselves to you, as you are to be a leader of the light workers and you need to see us. Others will perhaps have a more psychic human brain, which tunes into us better to the higher vibration and witnesses more of our realm.

We do sometimes reveal ourselves in times of great need too, if it is to prevent you passing home prematurely before your time is due, as you still have great purpose to achieve, and no life plan is perfect. Your lifeline will intertwine with thousands of others and sometimes unexpected things jump in; that is where we come in with your higher self, deciding whether to prevent this new interaction or let it play out. As you have free will, even with the best-set plans and intentions your life plans can go a little astray, so intervention from us is known. You are then left to go on your way again.

We have not prevented great wars and stopped mad men, we do not intervene in that way, as your world needs to play out and learn its own path to being as one. But we do nudge individuals gently on occasions to help them see the light, although it is still your free will to take that decision. All of you who have taken the step to the light have done so by free will and finding your inner essence, knowing you have love and light in your souls. Questioning this awakening is how you learn and grow towards a better world and us.

Don't be afraid to explore new possibilities in your lives, they are what will make you grow.

Dave - Why did you leave us so quickly?

Your life can be taken in the womb or you can live to a ripe old age – this is all planned before you come to earth. When a soul departs early the lesson is more for the loved ones left behind on earth; dealing with grief and loss helps you build inner strength, becoming stronger, quite often making you a better person and one day helping other people who are going through the same. The ones that depart early have fulfilled their life's journey, and return home to continue their spiritual learning.

John - What's it like where you are?

It is a place of beauty; you would feel as if you are floating on a cloud of love and peace in a magical world, and you would not want to return to anywhere else until you have absorbed its pure energy and love once again.

Mary - The existence of heaven & hell is always something, which I ponder upon. I wonder if the life that we are currently living on Earth is actually hell and when we die we are in heaven?

I always feel saddened when we hear a question like this. Your earth is a place of beauty; your life can be too. If your life is unhappy YOU can make the changes needed to improve it, and we will walk alongside you to help this happen; think of this when you feel down. The darkest hours some of you experience on earth can seem like what you call hell. But hell is what mankind has made; we have not created this for you. You can change this for yourself and others less fortunate. Let your children be the ones to do this. Teach them pure love ways and the dark will become light – don't live in the darkness.

Pirabu - "A soul can exist in different dimensions at the same time... The higher self knows this" ~ true or false?

The soul is your spirit and you can be on earth and in our spirit realm. Your higher self remains with us. We do not complicate things when this split occurs; the earth half remains where it is in your earth physical body until you come back home. As individuals we connect and work with one entity at a time. But your higher self will be in our realm, connecting with you on earth and they can pop to other places to observe as well.

Patricia - I believe that when we die our loved ones come to welcome us into the spirit world and we get to feel the love of the angels and god, but how come some spirits stay here on the earth plane? Why are there hauntings?

I love this question from Patricia, one we hear a lot amongst your conversations. When you pass over, your guardian angel and at least a couple of your spirit family meet you, but you have to be in acceptance of returning home with us. Sometimes, for example, when someone dies suddenly, or very young, or someone really doesn't believe in us, or strongly wants to get across a message to an earth loved one, they decide to stay earthbound for a bit. We do monitor them and eventually, when they are ready they come back home. Some are helped across to the light by your mediums and healers, or we collect them at an agreed time. Then there are some spirits who have lived dark lives on earth committing crimes against others, and don't want to face their loved ones back home; they, too, stay on the earth plane. Don't be freaked out, but in some circumstances, they can attach themselves to a human energy, which can affect the human's health and behaviour. This would need very experienced mediums to work with the human and spirit, to detach the spirit and ask them to return home.

Haunting is a word you use for spirit activity. Yes, spirits can try to get your attention if they are trying to give you a message. So beware of happenings around you after the passing of a loved one – they are trying to tell you something; it can be as simple as sorry, or I love you, or wanting to give healing messages to their loved ones. Go to a medium who is trusted, and the messages will come through. You can also get earthbound spirits who are mischievous and like to make you aware they are still on earth. As said above, they can be helped to cross over with an expert medium.

You can also get something that appears as haunting, but are actually memories captured in time and energy. Some more psychic people are more susceptible to these energies; they see them and feel them, while others can be in the same room and don't. Events or certain atmospheres can trigger them too, a bit like seeing an old film being triggered in the atmosphere.

Siobhan – I'm always wondering about the colour blue – it's a unique colour as it is transparent... colours fascinate me as there is a lot more to them than what we see everyday Xx

Blue is a colour we use with you for protection; it can also symbolise emotion in the throat chakra in Reiki healing. It is an uplifting colour – look at your beautiful blue earth skies and deep oceans, look upon it as an inspiration. We do not see it as cold; it's a colour of life, hope and purpose.

Maggie - We are beginning to see the return of the Divine Feminine. How can this be described to those who don't understand?

The Divine Feminine is an energy shift in the universe towards enlightenment in the 5th dimension. The energy becomes softer, more loving and forgiving, and helps you make the shift towards greater understanding, fewer wars, comforting your fellow man or woman like a mother does a child. Your mother earth's feminine energy will be listened to more.

More of you will believe in our realm and men amongst you will not be afraid to show their feminine side and more emotion and feelings. I'm sure as you read this you are aware that the new generation is showing signs of this. For example, the signs include acceptance of the gay and transvestite community, humans accepting each other as more and more of you open up your true selves and integrate into society as you should. You need to encourage mankind's enlightenment and bring this to your education system, bringing in teachings of holistic healing and meditations. These educated humans will be your new-inspired teachers for mankind to pass on their knowledge to your children.

Melanie – can a soul from another world or dimension merge with our soul while here on earth?

Thank you, my friend, for the forward-thinking question. We are aware of cases when this has happened. Our experience of this is it often causes an imbalance in the human body and mind. It can create a leader who will cause harm or destruction, or make a human mentally ill. The reason for this is the human body can only cope with so much. Quite often, the first soul from our spirit world will step aside in the body if the other energy is stronger, or there can be a switching back and forth in the mind, causing a dual personality. We do not intervene, but we do protect our Utopian spirit while this is in process; this situation also creates great educational learning points in your history and for us in Utopia.

Sophia – I wonder if those who have passed can see our souls completely, all our faults... and if they can forgive, or become angry or proud?

This questioned warmed my heart when I read it, as it is one I have wanted to answer for a while.

We can see your souls as your higher self monitors you. Your body energy and aura will show signs of illness or blockages. We know when you need healing and try to direct you to earth healers, your medical teams and holistic healers. As to faults that sit within your human mind and body, yes we are aware of them, as you are.

When you return home, we show no anger; forgiveness is for you to achieve from yourself in your healing time in our realm. Once this is done, you let go of any anger and hurt you collected on your life path, and you can celebrate what good you achieved. We do not see anything as failure, it is all lessons we learn, grow from and pass on to other Utopians. We can only show love and compassion.

Sam - I wonder if our loved ones can help to get rid of an unwanted energy? Thank you x

There are two answers to this question, depending on how you interpret it. Unwanted energy could be spirit around you; this is normally your loved ones, and you can ask them to step back and not be so noticeable, and they will oblige. Don't be afraid of them; they will be around you when you need them to guide and support you.

If you are feeling a lot of energy around you and feel as if you are buzzing on a high frequency, this could be your heightened self, so you need to come down to earth and be grounded. You can call up your guides to help you do this, or find a holistic healer, who could also help you. Walk in Mother Nature, feel your feet on her earth and breathe in her scents. Go to the ocean, walk on the sands and absorb Mother Earth's energy and strength.

Juanita - I often wonder about "AFTERLIFE" existence! Are those gone before us really "Dead"? Or in suspended animation? Watching our every move or guiding our

footsteps? It's a lot to think about huh?

You are right – there is a lot for mankind to think about. We have explained in an earlier chapter what happens when you pass over. Dead in your terms is the end of a physical body, but your spirit lives on in a very real existence in our realm. The millions of souls that have left your planet carry on living in our realm, while your organic body fades back to mother earth. Your spirit then exists in a different reality in Utopia, (see the first chapter). Some will come back to guide you and watch your life journey, others go to other places or stay in Utopia to fulfil their next chosen role.

Michelle - Do we need suffering to better understand and appreciate peace and everything good? Is that why this world can seem so cruel and unjust? And do we take our knowledge of our current lifetime back to spirit to learn from and ponder?

All the sufferings and cruelty you witness are of mankind's making; because of free will. As your spirit breaks through your human barriers and you are enlightened, these acts of unkindness will resonate with you more and more and you will want to stop or move away from them. This will help you on your road to the pure love and light, living all as one, in the peace you crave. Mankind can live in this existence of pure peace, we need you to teach this to all newborn children and as they grow up, so the cruelty in your world can end.

Debby - If we do not find our life purpose in this lifetime, would we have to reincarnate and experience a similar life in order to find it?

Your life purpose is the journey you map out for yourselves before you descend. Then, through enlightenment, you will mostly achieve this. Remember some of you will be here for a few days; others will stay for, say, 70 years or more of your time, all serving a purpose for the divine plan. One breath taken serves a purpose. You will have our teachings and lessons in Utopia to learn; as part of this, some of you choose to come to planets or realms and add to this knowledge, while others stay in Utopia all the time, developing within a chosen role, all as important as the next. Sometimes when you come home, you might decide to go back to complete your lessons. Or the lessons learned change your ideas and outlook, so the next life plan requirements alter, and you might want other lessons to learn. Continuous growth is our goal.

India - How does time run in heaven? I'm wondering if my baby will still be a baby or a grown-up lady when I join her? Xx

Babies passed over are pure early spirit, and when they come home the essence of who they were on earth will grow up in Utopia as part of the spirit. They are part of your soul group, so you will connect with them again on your return. The length of your lifetime on earth will depend how developed they have grown back home in Utopia. If you choose to visit a medium for a message, they will show themselves to the medium in their earth form when they passed, as well as the earth years of growth they would have reached at the time of the reading, so you can acknowledge and recognise them.

Caroline - Are there other energy beings apart from us? Do we have to reach a certain level spiritually before we become guides?

Yes, there are other beings and all life form is energy based, so I will break it down for you. The human organic life form and the Utopians' energy love and light source are two extreme examples. Between those extremes lie an abundance of various intelligent life forms, all at various levels of development. There is a vast universe out there made up of dimensions, planets and realms. We have been exploring over millennia of your years and still only touched on the tip of the iceberg as you humans say.

Utopians are all spiritual, and we grow stronger as we progress. We do have to have a high level of spirituality to be a guide, but a previous life on earth or other worlds or realms also helps us gain knowledge and experience. This in turn helps the guide who is overseeing you to help you at the best level they can. We love this role, because it helps who we are guiding to achieve the best from their experience on earth.

Mary - Do we choose our life experiences before we come to the earth plane?

When you decide on your life plan, you decide what lessons you would like to learn on this earth journey. You will expect to go through certain experiences from the knowledge we have learned from other visits. Your chosen lessons are included in the plan, but as you have free will, they might turn up at different times in your journey than we expected; and of course, you might also experience new ones. This always excites us, it's like a planned travel adventure – but always expect the unexpected! When you come back home we review it with each other, a bit like you would, reliving it through a slide show or photo album and telling your stories as you go.

Victor - Can our loved ones guide us when we are going through some very difficult times, and point us in the right direction, and how will I know?

Parted loved ones will guide you all your life and yes, they will send you messages for you to hear or see. But you have to be open to this, be accepting of the afterlife, and trust. Once you trust in us and ask, we will send guidance and messages by means of books, magazine, television and pictures. We also try to send messages mentally so if you get a repeating word or image in your head, please take notice of this. Once you accept we are there you will start to sense us, so ask us a question, trust the first thoughts you hear and use your intuition – it is our gift to you.

Release pain from your hearts so you can see,
the light on your path to travel your journeys'.

Alan - Why does it appear to be necessary to suffer so many trials and tribulations during one's life? Why the secrecy of not knowing our true existence?

Coming to earth is a challenge for us as mankind's ego is very destructive at the moment. All the trials and tribulations are your own making. Your challenge is to bring light and love to the dark corners of your world.

There is no secrecy – we exist and are happy to share this love and light with you all. Unfortunately, the majority of mankind have not been ready in their development and were not opening up to receive us. Even though millions worship in their religions, they do not feel and see us as those of you do that have now shed their shackles and been lifted higher into the love and light. But we are working very hard to change this with you and there has been a big shift in mankind opening up to enlightening your souls and giving more love to those around you and the world. We are also working through your children (there is more in the later chapters about this). Search out a spiritual church; these are growing in numbers everyday amongst you, so spread the word to your fellow mankind.

Cathy - Why do the Spirits not try to show themselves to us more so that thousands more would believe in the afterlife?

There is a balance to enlightening you and wanting you to believe, which is based on the level of mankind's development. If you open up and start to believe and develop trust in your spiritual journey, you will become more aware of us and see and feel more. When you start to communicate with us, for example as medium does, we will control this in your development as it uses your energy as well as energy around you, and can be draining. When mankind develops its psychic skills to a higher level this will not be an issue. If you are closed to us and we start popping up in front of you, you will be frightened, and we do not want this.

So there is a balance; mankind has to have faith and trust, develop spiritually, living an existence more in love and light. Once you become more enlightened, developed psychically and telepathically, you will have greater energy on a higher vibration; at that point, we will be a bigger part of your lives. This prospect really excites us.

Derek - What are spirits' thoughts on those aliens that have been to earth and do you have interactions with these aliens? Do they have your spirit in them?

We love this question as it shows someone who is thinking outside your day-to-day existence. As some of the pages in this book tell you, yes, aliens have been to Mother Earth many times and they still walk amongst you today. We know they have enhanced your societies and aided mankind's development, which we can only think of this as a good thing. Use your intelligent minds to seek out the footprints they have left for you.

Some of these species in the universe are highly intelligent, and have already reached the level of thinking we wish for mankind. Every being in your universe has a spark of the divine source, as we like to put it. This connects us all together, although we are all working at different levels. For example, the highly developed species tap into the universe's knowledge and are aware of us in the spirit realm all working for the greater good, and we work alongside them.

We are connected to other life forms in the way we are to you, too. We are learning, guiding, watching them develop wisdom, and moving towards love and light. They are at different levels of their development, some ascending to the 5th dimension, some as you were 10,000 years ago, and many in between.

We hear some of you talk about Star Seeds, some say this when various aliens species come and blend in your body's and memories wiped and then you live your life plan. There is confusion we are that's source but from one realm, and yes it is lovely to be thought of as star seeds as we come from the stars, we understand the thoughts behind this. Go to chapter 3, your path of Enlightenment for more information on alien interaction with your earth and remember Melanie's question.

Chris - What's a typical day in the world for spirit?

I love this question and I have decided to base it on mine. Well, we do not have day and night as you do, or breakfast and evening meals, but we do have structure and times when we gather to communicate and recharge our energy. My family spirit gathering is a key part of my day. This a chance to share knowledge, progress, welcome spirit family from their learning journeys and help others on their progress and development. In this time spent together, we look at our day-to-day roles, help that might be needed, and plan our next actions. Once this is all concluded, we will leave to the parts of our realm where we are needed and work. Work is a term I use for my role here; I do not earn a living, as we are all equal for our needs. We have no use for wealth such as money. We already have love and trust; our wealth is our knowledge and wisdom, our pure love and understanding.

I spend a lot of time in the knowledge library, overseeing our lessons and where developments are recorded. Our library is recorded in energy discs which look like large crystal spikes with energy running up and down them; these are all linked to our loving source of energy, which we can all tap into as needed.

I also tune into the earth soul I look after. I know when I am needed, and help and guide her, but I also help her team of guides and angels with her journey. I suppose we hold what you call meetings to discuss your life plans.

I will also sometimes meet with my own overseer about my own development and the next accession level I wish to reach. For yes, we do have ambition and dreams, but it is all for the good of each spirit in Utopia. I have others studying under me who I help teach to fill my role one day. I would like to be an overseer of the spirit families as a whole. This will take a lot of knowledge and growth, but as you say, I have time on my side. There is no rush in our world; all this happens in the thought of love and the greater good.

My recreational time as you have on earth, is taking time to look at our beautiful realm and appreciate its beauty and pureness. I also like to go to other places we visit; I am studying to add to our knowledge pot. I have reached the part of my development where I now have greater freedom and am trusted to explore these exciting worlds. They will not know I'm there in their worlds; as my all-knowing skills develop, I can now be there with them with a thought.

I do not have material possessions as you do; if I were to declare one in earthly terms, my wisdom would be my greatest possession. We share love for all Utopians, but I do have a stronger bond with my spirit family group, with whom I have spent longer than any other Utopians.

Chapter 3

Your path of Enlightenment

The Universe is yours, go out into the endless space and search for the wisdom and knowledge you seek

Your earth's history is full of stories of visitors from other worlds; the evidence collected by mankind is engraved in drawings on the walls of ancient civilizations, through to images captured by modern day mankind. This has influenced you in your development and your views on your mortality. There have been suggestions that your gene pool has been influenced by off-world visitors too; this did take place at various times between 20,000 to 3,000 years ago.

UFOs visit your world and have done so for centuries. Off-world civilisations have lived amongst you for a while, influencing your world. For example, the myths and stories of the Atlantans are based on extra-terrestrial facts. Your world has known great civilizations from beyond, but the power of Mother Earth has often bought them to their knees, or they have chosen to return home, leaving behind hardly any evidence that they were there. But as well as looking on your earth's surface or on nearby planets, you must also look deep into your oceans and lakes, as there is another world unexplored and much to be revealed to you. Look below you, as well as to the stars. Your ocean is a great hiding place and extra-terrestrials can use the water mass like a reflector to hide themselves. The oceans cover more than 71% of your planet and is a vast and largely unexplored world, still a mystery to you all.

We do not want to put fear into you, but extra-terrestrials do come amongst you today, as we do. They also travel by dimensional methods, from solar systems to other solar systems, covering great distances in unimaginable crafts. And just to blow your mind further, we visit some of them for our further advancement, as we do your planet. If you look how your technology has advanced in the last 70 years, it has an off-planet earth influence. Your leaders do hide a lot of evidence of UFOs, due to fear of how your society will deal with this knowledge; but as you are advancing toward enlightenment about all things, mankind is experiencing a shift of expectancy and sharing knowledge, and it's time for you to stand up and ask for this knowledge.

If you think of how we connect with you, we are on a higher frequency; you can't see or hear us until you raise your energy frequency and we drop ours down nearer to yours. We can then communicate. WOW. So think: this can work with other dimensions, realms and beings. A lot of other species have mastered this in their evolution; humans are just a couple of hundred years behind. Within yourselves, you have the power to travel in your minds, as well as physically, to these worlds. You have already worked out the universe is made of energy, as all of us are. No other species is different; all have the Divine universal energy base, each of you just formed in a different way. It's awesome. I wish you could see what I have seen.

Off-world visitors have influenced mankind over the centuries; some of your greatest artists, philosophers, inspirers and inventors have had connection with unseen influence that has made them ahead of their time – Leonardo De Vinci, Albert Einstein and Isaac Newton are just a few examples.

I feel a great example is Leonardo De Vinci, born in your year of 1452; he was what you call a genius of his time. He was a painter, architect, inventor, and student of all things scientific. Today, you know him best for his art, including two paintings that remain among the worlds most famous and admired. He was largely self-educated, and he filled dozens of secret notebooks with inventions, observations and theories about pursuits from aeronautics to anatomy. The rest of the world was just starting to share knowledge in books, and most people found the concepts expressed in his notebooks were often difficult to interpret. As a result, though he was recognised in his time as a great artist, his contemporaries often did not fully appreciate his genius. Leonardo was capable of tapping into the universe's knowledge, and the combination of psychic intellect and imagination allowed him to create, at least on paper, such inventions as the bicycle, the helicopter and an airplane based on the physiology and flying capability of a bat. But as you will know from reading your history, mankind was not ready for these inventions and theories; Leonardo was simply too advanced for his time.

I would also like to mention your Nostradamus, born on December 14th 1503, one of your world's most famous authors of prophecies. He had quite a psychic mind and tapped into universal knowledge, foreseeing future events with 'mind time travel'. Your future is not set in stone, and although future scenarios can be seen by minds like his and ours, mankind can alter your futures with their actions. I only wish you could see what we see, so that this would become clear. Mankind makes his future. Also take note of Nostradamus's predictions on UFO encounters; a lot of his predictions came true, and so will others. Take the time to read about him – you will be enlightened and fascinated by his life and predictions. But don't let this cause you stress, as futures can be altered by a shift to the light and living as one. Don't let your imagination run away with you.

Talking of imagination, I also love your Star Trek films where your imagination and longing to explore the universe has created these scripts, where the characters visit other solar systems but are not allowed to interfere in the prime directive. This was our aim as we started on our quest, but as you became more aware that there was more to you than a flesh shell, our connection with you got stronger, and we have influenced your societies, religions and beliefs, although not intentionally. We have also intervened for the greater good of mankind.

One of the visiting off-world species I would like to tell you about are called Drygonmi; they came to earth in spaceships, giving knowledge and wisdom to mankind. They are smaller than humankinds, with a skin that you would think of as a lizard texture, with human form – four limbs and a head, just like you. They come from a highly advanced, peaceful world, travelling the universe as explorers. They communicated to you telepathically when they arrived. Influences are in the advancement of the Greek and Roman culture around 3000-4000 years ago, which spread across your lands and influenced other cultures. Now ask yourselves: where did the Greek and Roman gods come from? In Greek mythology you have tales of heroes, gods and demigods that walk among mortals, have great powers, great knowledge and are capable of saving or destroying mankind. But these tales go beyond your Greek mythology; all over the world there are amazing tales of Heroes and Gods and in all of those tales, these mythological creatures are described as having powers beyond human capabilities. The Drygonmi will return one day and watch from afar. Don't fear, my friends; this is no different to what we do from our realm.

Time travel is possible amongst some off-world civilizations; I know mankind dreams of this from your films and stories. If mankind opened their minds' eye a little more you would be amazed at what's going on around you; just imagine it is not just your world they travel to, but to many other worlds, realms and dimensions too.

Some extraterrestrials navigate by the star systems; over the millions of years, stars and galaxies shift in the universe and the night skies. If you could go back across that time period, the sky of stars would be so different. Mankind has also used the stars to guide them around the planet earth, which helped you to discover that your earth was round, not flat. Look how far you have come since then. The reason I mentioned the stars is that the aliens who have been amongst you built structures aligned with the stars and their home planets. They left you a lot of evidence of how to find their homes. One day you will reach out to them, then our knowledge and discovery with you will really take on a new meaning and dimension of learning. We look forward to this day.

Remember the moment in your Star Trek movies, when the Vulcans come to earth in peace because earth technology has made a massive breakthrough; fiction is nearer to the truth in your universe than you imagine. Know that there is a universal galactic order of super-intellect beings, from other worlds and dimensional realms, which are peace loving and highly developed on all fronts. They are waiting for earth to take that next leap in evolution, and hoping you do not destroy yourselves first. They want you to join them. Well, this is a reality already. Mankind has already been contacted by off-world civilisations, and governments and religious sects have so much evidence. But to be part of the amazing secrets of the universe, mankind needs to ascend to the next stage of development. You are being gently aided but we feel you need our pure love input to make the breakthrough.

There are two ways in which mankind can achieve enlightenment. The first one will happen through destroying and polluting your world to the point where Mother Nature reacts to cleanse herself; the human population that survives will then live a cleansed, new existence, their future history pages remembering how mankind destroyed themselves. They will cast off their old ways, learning to live in a caring and balanced way, rebuilding their lives and civilisations over centuries, in a loving and enlightened way. No more mixed religion, no more wars, and harmony amongst men. We believe you will tap into greater inner strength and use your psychic abilities to your full potential. Over time, you will jump from the third dimension to the fifth. A lot of the survivors will be light workers who will teach and pass on their healing knowledge and ways of thinking to mankind. It is only at this point of self-destruction that you will listen, if your past history is anything to go by.

The second way mankind could save yourselves is to *STOP NOW* and look at the way you live. Look at what you are doing to Mother Earth and listen to her, she is crying out in pain to you – please take heed of her pain. Search the planet for messages left by earlier off-world civilizations, and discover your full potential this way. The revelations are not for the few; this is for all of mankind. Your top governments have already discovered some secrets and try to use them in technology, so they are one step ahead of the rival countries that they feel threatened by, but these discoveries could be used to help and heal your planet. If the truth of alien intervention was revealed, followers of religious sects would question their beliefs, and religions do not want to be threatened, as they have built up great wealth. But this is not the right way forward for mankind. Mankind will realise one day that there has been off-world intervention, and that there is one high pure loving energy source – only one GOD.

If I were in your shoes, I would choose the second option. But for either option to be a success, you need to discover how to use your brain to its full potential; it is so much more advanced than you realise, and there is so much universal knowledge to tap into. How to rise above the mentality of war, hate, rivalry and jealously of others? You could develop your psychic abilities to raise your intelligence a thousand-fold, then mankind will fly to the stars, visit other dimensions and tap into the mass of wisdom and knowledge available to them.

How are we helping you?

We are working with you to develop more light workers to spread the word and faith amongst you, in the hope this leads you to the second option mentioned earlier. More of you opening up to love will aid your planet and help the shift towards a better world.

Spiritualism is the way forward for mankind; we are not doing this just by bringing this in to your existing religions, but through new spirit churches, and other similar groups that are forming. This is a gradual process and a big task, but we see a light at the end of the tunnel. The reason we are not concentrating on the religious sectors so much is that they are so divided and corrupt in their way of thinking. Some religions run their faiths by fear, not love. What do we mean by fear? *"There is no fear in love, but perfect love casts out fear; for fear has to do with punishment, and whoever fears, has not reached perfection in love."* From your bible -1 John 4:18. Fear... it is just a word, but religions that have lost their way use it as a controlling device to get people to do what they want; this is not a good base for any faith. Living honest, positive, true values, and lifestyles spreading love and light in a non-fearful way, is the only faith you all need.

Spiritualism has now progressed in modern mankind to the point that it is now classed as a religion, so it can be recognised by the powers that be. We accept this in Utopia, as this will help the message spread out to your world; one day, this will be the true faith of mankind, all living as one.

You are all one as we are; this is the message we need convey to mankind. Once this happens, all religions will work alongside each other, some dissolving into a loving, non-fearing belief system, and mankind will rise to the next level of development and ascension.

I discuss spirituality deeper further on, but wanted you to know how Utopians have decided to work with you at the moment. But as mankind has free will, we have to sit back and wait to see the outcome, giving gentle nudges and signs in the hope you see them and act. This book is one of those.

You are being watched by us as observers, but also by other off-world civilizations, to see how you develop and progress on your planet's path. When the time is right they will appear again to you, when you are ready to learn further from them, as we will. You need to believe in yourselves and have faith to take that next leap in your evolution my friends.

Look for messages from the stars

Reach for the stars
Reach for the top of the highest mountain
Reach for the top of the highest trees
Reach beyond your wildest dreams
Reach into your heart for strength
Reach to your higher self for guidance
Never look down, never look back
Just reach for your dreams,
they are within your grasp.

Humans have walked the earth for an estimated 200,000 of your earth years, slowly developing and being visited by off-world civilisations. Throughout your centuries are drawings, paintings, carvings, buildings and markings that have depicted off-world visits; these are found all over the world. There are also recorded photos, videos, text in your manuscripts, books and online data, and file upon file of government evidence! And don't forget the humans amongst you who have been taken by off-world species then returned, and those of you who stay off-world to this day.

Your books and online Internet world are full of stories and images of this evidence. Here is a list of some facts I have gathered from your Earth knowledge pot for you to absorb, of evidence of UFOs across your world. We have asked these to be added as glimpses of proof for you that are right under your nose. We know this will stimulate you to seek further knowledge from your books, in your world and on your Internet. Evidence is also on your earth's surface, under your oceans and on nearby planets.

Your art depicts UFOs from other worlds

Art throughout your centuries depicts aliens and UFOs. Here are a few samples of what you have found; this is just the tip of the iceberg, so go off and investigate the examples given below, you will find it fascinating. Mankind needs to be more curious, to find out about your past and to secure your future. Look across your continents and societies new and old – every country has all of this evidence.

The Lolladoff Plate is a 12-thousand year old stone dish that was found in Nepal. The pattern on the central disc spirals out from a sun, out of which there seems to appear a reptile, followed by a spaceship, followed by bacteria or atom designs, and then a reptile on the outer edge; at the centre of it all is a figure believed to represent an alien.

In Kimberley, Australia, c3000 B.C.: These cave drawings are thought to be spirit beings represented as giant humanoid figures, some measuring close to 23 feet tall. They have grey alien-like eyes, cone-shaped heads, and no mouth or ears. These drawings look much like beings in helmets, or with physical qualities that are not human.

In the Sego Canyon c. 3000-5000 B.C.: In the state of Utah, USA, are the cave paintings created by Anasazi and Fremont Native Indians. These paintings show strange beings with exaggerated eyes, large craniums and physical size, (they are similar to Australia's spirit beings). The Indians believe these drawings are the star people, the beings that came from the heavens to create people, and then returned from whence they came.

Saqqara, Egypt: There is evidence in some of your old civilisations that the modern medicine of your day was practiced thousands of years ago. In Saqqara lies the Physician's Tomb - also known as the Tomb of Ankhmahor, it was built more than 4,000 years ago for one of the most important officials of the ancient Egyptian civilisation. The physician Ankhmahor performed very complex surgical and medical procedures according to the drawings found. There is evidence of a circumcision, reflexology, an operation on the hands; they may also have had brain surgery removing tumours. Their stories say they got their knowledge from Thoth, the god of wisdom and science, who brought to them all the knowledge from the gods in one complete package, rather than something that developed out of a society that before then, had been extremely primitive. According to your ancient stories, this divine physician healed the eye of the Egyptian god Horus after his uncle Set gouged it out in an epic battle for power. As a result, the Eye of Horus became an important symbol of restoration and good health. Look into this story, as there are other Gods mentioned who came from the stars.

Egyptian Pictograph, 400 B.C.: As part of this wall art, a caped alien is offered some sort of live fowl. The Egyptian people also seemed to be well equipped with deep knowledge and understanding about outer space. There are actually spiral images in the Egyptian hieroglyphics, which mean galaxies, energy, etc. Aside from that, there are images of some half-animal, half- human creatures, as well as reptilian creatures. Some of you actually think that these are images and symbols of extra-terrestrials, and you would be correct in thinking they influenced this. There are images from a 3,000-year old 'New

Kingdom Temple' in Egypt which also show some images of the modern day submarines, helicopters, and something that looks like a UFO on the ceiling.

Peruvian Hill Carving, 6th Century: There is a figure of alien form carved into the side of a hill.

Pakal's tomb 683 A.D.: The design and engineering of Pakal's tomb are very similar to the Egyptian pyramids. The lid on the tomb of 'Pakal' tomb describes how his soul would return to the stars, from where he came. It shows the ruler seated upon the "Monster of the Sun". This term and the carving are clearly trying to communicate that Pakal took off from earth in a spacecraft. The primitive Mayans were using words they understood and images that aimed to represent what they saw. One can understand how a primitive Mayan would describe a rocket ship blasting off as a monster. The blinding light of the engine exhaust as the rocket hurtled into space would look like the sun. Hence the monster of the sun. Interesting is it not?

In the year 776, a flying object was sighted during the siege of the Castle Sigiburg, in France. There are two illustrations of the incident on a twelfth-century manuscript, *"Annales Laurissenses"*. Another UFO shape appears in the Notre-Dame Basilica Tapestry.

11th century example: Painting on the interior wall of 'The Svetitskhoveli Cathedral' shows two UFOs flying away.

1327-Visoki Decani Monastery: Again, The Crucifixion of Christ, as seen in the Sventiskhoveli Cathedral, shows two flying objects in the upper left and right of the scene, piloted by beings that appear to be holding steering controls. Or are they futuristic time travellers, stopping by to see one of the major events in world history? All these are influenced by stories of visitors from outer space and other dimensions, with mankind's interpretation reflected in the paintings.

The Annunciation with Saint Emidius, 1486: The Annunciation celebrates the announcement of Gabriel to Mary that she would conceive the Son of God. Mankind has always said that Mary got pregnant without conception; alien intervention has happened across mankind's history, and this is one of your stories linked with this intervention. In the picture, alien saucers shoot light beams, which impregnated Earth women. It's interesting how these space ships keep popping up in mankind's interpretations of the stories in art. Also remember Jesus' healing powers, his empathy and kindness; he descended from the heavens and was different to all other men. Mankind was not ready for this new age man, as you had not developed enough on your spiritual path, and the powerful, greedy and scared humans still in control, out-weighed heavily those of you who were starting to see the light back then. We are glad to say the balance today favours the change needed for you to ascend to where you need to be.

1561 - Battle of Nuremberg: The original woodcut print by Hans Glaser, of the residents of Nuremberg, who saw what was described as an aerial battle of strange flying objects that flew with vapour trails and wielded spears at each other. This battle was followed by the appearance of a large black triangular object that crashed outside the city. According to eyewitnesses, there were hundreds of spheres, cylinders and crosses engaged in the battle.

In one of the oldest churches of Russia, **in Svetitskhoveli, in Georgia**, you can see a fresco, dated from the 17th century, where, on each side of the cross, one can distinguish two flying objects, inside each of which a face looks at the scene of the crucifixion.

In 1710, a painting by well-known and Vatican-connected artist Aert de Gelder showed a UFO illuminating the baptism of Christ. There were other paintings showing Jesus Christ and UFOs in art, but when the French revolution came this subject was beginning to be a threat to your Vatican (your people before this time were uneducated and not interested in art and paintings, except in the Renaissance period, when paintings featuring UFOs were particularly present). All artwork started to be censored, and any work that threatened the Vatican and its religious dogma were seized and banned.

In 1803, the Legend of Utsuro Bune (Hollow Ship) in Japan was recorded in drawings, this story of a ship washed up on the shores of Japan. In this UFO was a young woman, depicted holding a box, the drawings tell this story. My friends, please search out the rest of this story.

In **Salamankindca Cathedral Church**, an image of what appears to be an astronaut is carved into the stone of a pillar. This work was started in the 1600s and finished in the 1800s.

As well as art, pottery figures have been found, depicting what look like men in space suits. Some have been found in Ecuador and in Kiev, dated to around 4,000 BC.

This is just small amount of worldwide art evidence to show how in times past, people believed that men who have gone before and walked amongst you, were from the stars. Over the last few centuries, religious sects have suppressed these stories, but as you have shifted into your new century, all the old veils are being lifted and mankind can no longer suppress this in the parts of the world that have freedom of speech. Once the whole world sees this message and all have freedom of speech, you will make the breakthrough you need.

Alien building blocks

As well as art, there are ancient structures across the world that baffle mankind. The precision of them, the engineering way beyond human capabilities of that time, suggest they were helped by alien civilisations over the centuries. Some are on land, and some are under the sea. A lot of them are built in alignment with the stars; these were guides for off-world beings, as well as footprints left for mankind to follow them home one day.

Again, I have selected a few examples to inspire you to look further into your planet's history.

Tiwanaku is a Pre-Columbian archaeological site in western Bolivia, South America. It was the capital of an empire that extended into your present-day Peru and Chile, the estimated 14,000- year old crumbled buildings still show geometrically perfect shapes which will amaze you, as the pre-Columbian people that inhabited this region had no written language and still used stone and bronze tools; you have to question how they built these amazing structures. Even after years of outdoor erosion, you can still see the perfectly shaped stones, intricately routed patterns and perfectly drilled round holes of alien technology origins.

Yonaguni Monument: This underwater mystery off the coast of Japan features pillars, a road, a star-shaped platform and other relics of man-made architecture. The ruins date back to at least 5,000 years, based on the dates of stalactites found inside underwater caves that sank with the city. Again, in this period mankind could not have built the structure alone.

On Bimini Road, North Bimini Island in the Bahamas, lie three peculiar straight stretches of "road." Each is composed of hundreds of large rectangular blocks. The main structure stretches linearly for a great distance before disappearing into the sea. This baffles mankind again what was it used for? Where does it lead? Some of you believe that this was part of the road system of the lost continent of Atlantis.

Rock UFO: Off the coast of Stockholm in the Baltic Sea, 1912 ocean divers discovered an object made of rock-like substance that could not be explained; it is believed to be a possible ancient UFO.

The Trilithon is just your regular old everyday temple to the gods in Lebanon. It's not that exciting, except that the temple is built on three shaped stones that are some of the most massive pieces of building material in the world. The three stones used in the temple base measure 290 feet long and 160 feet wide and weight an astonishing 750-800 tons each. Nearby, in a quarry, sits an unused stone that weighs 1200 tons. That's the weight of 3 passenger airplanes. How did these ancient masons (maybe Roman, but speculated to be much older than your Roman occupation) cut, transport, and lift these massive stones on top of other stones weighing 350 tons each? Makes mankind question and think!!!

The Nazca Lines: Amongst the Nazca lines are big shapes of monkeys and hummingbirds. Their purpose can't be explained readily, but you know how they were made: you figure out a shape and dig until you get to the different coloured rock. What is really interesting are the straight lines criss-crossing the plains. These stretch for up to 15 miles in some cases, but remain perfectly straight the entire way across, some as deep as 24 inches, and perfectly formed. One of mankind's theories is that stakes were connected at either end with something stretched across, and these stakes have even been "found," but carbon dated to after the time the lines were thought to have been drawn. Also – what could be produced by ancient Peruvian peoples and then stretched for over a mile? And only be appreciated as a straight line from the air? Food for thought!! Many of you believe this is aliens at work again, creating landing strips seen from space and other dimensions. Your earth book 'Chariot of the Gods' will make interesting reading for you. Also look at sun, star and mandalas, which are found in ancient messages for mankind in Nazca and other parts of the world to this day. And don't forget your modern day crop circles – there are lots of circles and similar designs all round the world.

Remember, there are hidden messages on the ground, on the walls and under the seas.

The Palpa Flat Mountain: Another mystery of Nazca is the flat-topped mountain a few miles away from the lines. High above the plain, and marked with some of the thicker lines, there is an enormous mountain with a perfectly flat top. Mankind believes it's very possible that the top of this mountain was completely sheared off by something (or someone) to make this a level surface to carve more lines on. But no debris from this earth movement is found scattered around the mountain. But large piles of stone are scattered around the plateau and they are organised piles, which, when connected like a "connect the dots book," are believed to be Phoenician writing – from across the Atlantic Ocean. More food for thought for mankind, and bits of the puzzles yet unanswered.

The Mayans used to construct one pyramid over another. In the site at Calakmul, rooms were discovered inside the pyramid, alongside finds that clearly depict UFOs and alien life forms. This civilisation had monolith-type structures and were an amazing advancement for primitive mankind. They foretold events in mankind's history, including the belief that the aliens would return. Since your year 2012, there has been a massive energy shift towards these UFO beliefs, and believing in our realm. The Mayans predicted a massive change on earth; it was not the end of your world, as mankind believed, but it is the road to enlightenment. This is the start of a new era for mankind, which will build steadily over time. Mankind just has to make the right choices to thrive and tune into great knowledge, as the Mayans did.

Underground tunnels that go round the world: In 2003, mankind used ground-breaking radar in unexplored areas of your world to discover a complex system of labyrinthine underground tunnels and structures. Some of these tunnels, leading to other parts of the world, have been discovered at places like the Bucegi Mountains in Romania, Guatemala in South America, and tunnels have been mapped under the Mayan pyramid complex at Tikal, and in Baghdad, Iraq. These most remarkable discoveries were made thanks to mankind's technology. Within some of these structures, energy field barriers were in place, only some of which could be penetrated. Artefacts and unexplained items were also found. Please, my friends, research these stories – you will find them fascinating. Where has the evidence gone? Look underground!

Monoliths have been found round your world, in most of your civilisations. They started appearing a lot on your earth around 3-4,000 years ago. All are part of ancient systems of worship, with most of them aligning with the sun and stars. You have to ask what made these civilisations, which had no contact with each other, start building these structures and worshipping the heavens? There are even off-world planets like your moon and Mars that hold secrets in your solar system. But you will find more under your oceans. Some Monoliths are engraved with ancient messages; they were built in your ancient cities, or outside formal areas of worship. A lot of the ancient buildings take a monolithic form. Search your earth's knowledge pot for them: 'The Stellae of Axum' in Ethiopa; Karnak and Heliopolis in Egypt; 'Le Grand Menhir Brise' in Brittany, France; The 'Lateran' Obelisk in Rome; 'Tlaloc Statue' in Mexico; 'Gate of the Puma' in Tiahuanaco; Easter Island; The 'Gollenstein' in Germany; 'The Cove', Avebury, and 'Stonehenge' in England; 'Old Keig' in Scotland; and 'Gobekli Tepe' in Turkey.

Also on Easter Island, man has recently discovered the monoliths are over thousands of years old, a lot older than first thought. The faces carved on them, also appear on monoliths in other parts of the world. They are thought to reflect the faces of the civilisation that carved them. There are hundreds of monoliths around your world, some yet to be discovered. Study them and the carved messages and secrets within will be revealed.

A lot of answers will also come from deep oceans and your seabeds; for years, your Bermuda Triangle has caused wonder and unanswered questions. Also be aware of discoveries that appear in the news, then are easily forgotten or rumoured to be fakes; some of the evidence is being destroyed or hidden by the powerful governments afraid of what you would make of the evidence left behind for mankind to discover. As you are starting to fight for your wildlife's survival, fight for these governments to reveal their secrets and fund exploration. You need to ignite a course of action – don't wait for others to start this, be a leader.

Your world's history stories hold the secrets

Your written books of old, such as your Bibles stories, tell of mankind's interaction with the being that you call God. Your various languages define the meaning of this word in various ways, as creator, ruler, superhuman being or spirit or divine. God derives from the old word Good in your English language. Some of you say 'Lord God' – in general, 'Lord' means overseer of lands, dominant, noble, ruler and so on... Across your world, whatever the word used for God in different languages, it has derived from the stories of mankind worshipping unexplained beings from the stars, and glimpses of the pure love of our realm.

Amongst the Bible stories, the one that stands out to me is the Story of Moses. This is a good example; the story depicts a burning bush, the chariot of fire, rising to the gods, descending from and rising in whirlwinds from heaven – these are good descriptions of off-world visitors. There's also the story of Jesus, the guiding star, descending from heaven and rising back to heaven. In the Moses story, Moses disappears for 40 days and 40 nights; on his return, his appearance had altered – he was recognised as Moses, but a change had come over him, which mesmerised mankind. On his return from his disappearance, he brought guidance for peace and harmony amongst men. This is an old story that fits in with your earth claims of abductions, being taken by off-world beings. But have faith, my friends, and no fear, as all these interventions have been done in peace and love, wanting to guide mankind and influence your world for the better.

Another story from your bible is that of Jonah and the whale. This could be read as abduction: he was taken by a vessel from the sea depths, it was a shiny bronze colour and said to be a whale. Remember, the people who witnessed it did not understand what they saw, so they would only be able to describe things they could relate to, as you would today if you saw an unidentified object. A very basic example for you; if you saw a circle object in the sky with a long stick type object sticking out of its side, you could describe it as a saucepan shape – see what I mean?

Another quick example is the book of Enoch, written thousands of years ago, which tells of fallen angels and suggested tales of aliens, gods descending to earth and fire in the sky; in common with all of your ancient literature, the evidence of off-world intervention lies in its pages. Enoch was taken away from the planet by a fire god: *"With fiery horses appeared in a whirlwind, and Enoch ascended into heaven."* seek these books out; it is for you to read and find the evidence mankind needs to be inspired.

In India, scripts from over 4,000 years old have been studied. A small example is the Ramayana writings, in which the text describes space vehicles similar to the so-called flying saucers reported throughout your world today. The Ramayana even describes a beautiful chariot which "arrived shining, a wonderful divine car that sped through the air". There is mention of a chariot seen *"sailing overhead like a moon"*, and another passage says: *"At Rama's behest, the magnificent chariot rose up to a mountain of cloud with a tremendous din."* Then there is:

"Bhima flew with his Vimana on an enormous ray which was as brilliant as the sun and made a noise like the thunder of a storm."

I would also like to include this example from your earth's great continent, China. It is the story of the first Emperor of China, Huang-Di (2697-2598 B.C.) or *"The Yellow Emperor,"* and the ancestor of all Chinese. The stories describe him as a *"son of heaven"*. According to legend, before Huang-Di was born there was "a radiance from the great star Chi and the Dipper Constellation" (Ursa Major). His conception was marked by a *"thunderclap on a clear day in the skies"*. Your stories reveal that he brought traditional Chinese Medicine (including acupuncture) to the country. His wife taught the Chinese how to make silk, which was also believed to come from the stars. He was said to live in the Kunlun-Mountains, which are in the heart of Tibet. After he lived and ruled for over 100 years, he is said to have prepared his "return to the skies". Then a metallic dragon *"descended from the sky and took Huang-Di away"*. This is yet another earth story reflecting intervention by off-world civilisations.

This story from Chinese mythology is like so many other ancient accounts of gods and half-gods, told across your earth over centuries. In ancient texts, nearly every country on your earth has stories of mankind and gods in flying machines. A lot of UFO activity has been recorded in your books, mankind perceiving them as gods. We have witnessed earth's interactions and how your free will interrupted them. It is understandable that unusual beings outside your understanding would be perceived as gods. Yes, they were and are more powerful than you, but they are not the source of love and light, what all mankind seeks.

The other evidence is left written on relics in shapes or ancient languages. A quick example is the cone-shaped gold hats with moon symbols and stars, which were found across Europe. They hold a mathematic table too advanced for what you thought mankind was capable of; they were believed to be worn by priests to speak to the high divine (metal is a conductor for energy). Where do I stop? This book could be filled with evidence.

I will finish with glimpse of the giant gods mentioned throughout your ancient world literature, including the bible. (And remember the wall art In Kimberly, Australia, and Sego Canyon, USA). One of the ancient stories is about the Annunaki from around 3,600 years ago of your time. They were giant hominoids, believed to have visited your Earth from their home planet, standing on average eight foot tall, and far heavier and more muscular than humans. Mankind thought them to be from other worlds and worshipped them as gods who brought technology and wisdom. They were believed to have come from a dying 12th planet Nibiru, and came here to mine gold. Mixing with mankind, as well as using them to mine, they passed on their genes and knowledge.

There have been stories of giants across your world – the United States, Solomon Islands and Peru are just a few examples, all dating back to this time period. You have to think about where they came from, and for what purpose, as they were not from earth. Evidence such as large bones, large tools and footprints in stone have been found, as well as drawings and stories. A lot of evidence has been blocked or lost, but mankind is unearthing more and more; again, my friends, browse your Internet and books for the evidence and ask your governments questions, as these stories all stem from ancient truths.

Life is a fragment of time, healing is a moment of time.

Time travel

There is also evidence in your ancient texts of time travel, or off-world visits to other realms and dimensions, from people who return to your planet a long time later. Some of you would say they are ancient myths and legends; I can tell you these are all based on facts of their times, but as with all your ancient and modern texts, mankind can use their free will and decide after looking at all the evidence. Please remember your modern day Albert Einstein, who published his special "Theory of Relativity" in 1905 & 1916. According to his astonishing scientific breakthrough, space and time are one, opening the page for many questions such as: *"Time travel – a possibility?"* The story 'The Time Machine' preceded this theory written by HG Wells and first published in 1895 and was then in 1960 turned into a film that inspired and set your imaginations alight.

If you look back into very ancient texts, you will find the Japanese legend of Urashima Taro. He was said to visit the underwater palace of the Dragon God Ryujin. He stayed there for three days, but when he returned to the surface, 300 years had passed. Everything that he knew of was long gone, his family, friends and his way of life – everything had changed in what seemed to be for him only a few days.

In the Buddhist text, Pali Canon, it is written that in the heaven of the thirty Devas (the place of the gods), time passes at a different pace, and one hundred Earth years count as a single day for them. In the ancient Indian text of the Mahabharata, written in the eighth century BC, King Raivata is described as travelling to the heavens to meet with the creator god Brahma, only to return to Earth hundreds of years in the future.

I have another story for you. During the persecutions under Decius (c.250), when Christians were in dispute with the Roman state, seven young men went into a cave where they fell asleep. When they woke up, they wandered into the city of Ephesus to buy food. They were astounded when they learned that they had slept not for one night but for two hundred years, and that Christianity had spread to every corner of the Roman Empire. When Emperor Theodosius II heard the incident, he accepted it as evidence of resurrection, which was being discussed in the churches then. The sleepers later died naturally and were buried in the cave in which they had slept.

In your modern times, top scientists are working both openly and secretly on time travel. At the University of Connecticut, a theoretical physicist has created a large-scale model of a time machine. Using a device called a ring laser that produces a circulating beam of light, he hopes to prove that the twisting light actually bends space, forming a loop in time. Fascinating – mankind will time travel one day of their own accord!

As you interacted with off-world beings over time, and learned of your soul's existence, spirit and our love all around you, the two have combined into your books of worship, with your various world civilizations all writing their own stories around events in their part of the world. Study, my friends, you will see that a lot of the off-world interventions happened in the same time periods. They were recorded in your stories, and in ancient times, they were recorded in your wall art.

History of your world's medicine and healing

Mankind's modern medicine and the technology have really progressed in the last 50 years. Holistic and spiritual healing has been used by some of earths Eastern civilisations for centuries. In the last 20 years, holistic and spiritual healing is more widely used now by your western civilisations, and in the last couple of years in your hospitals. This is a great leap forward for mankind.

The oldest documentation of holistic healing are drawings depicting the practice of reflexology, discovered in the tomb of an Egyptian physician, Ankhmahor, dated around 2,500 BC. Within this tomb were found many medically related paintings; the most famous pictures from Ankhmahor's Tomb are in the doorway to the Pillared Hall. These are the medical scenes that show representations of surgical procedures, including the circumcision of a priest, which is comparable to a similar relief in the Temple of Mut at Karnak in Luxor, from a much later date. Another relief shows a foot operation being performed - sited by many reflexologists as proof of ancient alternative therapies practiced on both the hands and feet.

Other evidence is found in earth's ancient bones. Around your world, unusual bones and skulls have been found, and after study, the elongated skulls are thought to be not human. Skeletons have also been found of the giant humanoid forms we mentioned earlier. The DNA of these findings, yet to be revealed, holds the secrets, my friends.

I will like to highlight awareness around the use of Holistic healing and Mother Earths natural remedies for mankind. As long as you carry on pumping manmade chemicals in your selves and Mother Earth and her environment, the more of earth that man destroys the less natural remedies there are for you all. It is like you are swimming against a heavy current, wading through all this to create some good. The scales of balance need to be tipped. FLIP that coin, pursue the holistic way of life, every little bit of progress will tip the scales. Fight against pollution and what man is doing to your Planet, YES your planet, your home.

Off-world communication with numbers - The Universal 3

Trinity in your world.

Other ways that off-world species can communicate with you are through maths and numbers. Have you ever thought, as you all took your maths lessons, how mathematics connects you to many off-world species – it's not your everyday thought, is it? Fundamentally, basic maths is a way to connect with them. I'll use one number for an example – the number three. For a long time, this number has shown up across your world as objects appearing in threes. This number works well in the third dimension's way of thinking and communication.

So when you exist in what you call the third dimension, you do things in threes so they will manifest in your physical realm. Three is the first number to which the meaning "all" was given. It is The Triad, being the number of the whole, as it contains the beginning, middle and end. The use of three has been given to your use of words when reflecting on religions and the deep meanings of your world. Notice how mankind has used three words to sum up life in these examples: 'heaven, earth and waters'; to be human - body, soul and spirit, or birth, life and death; past, present and future.

The symbol of three is a triangle. Look at your triangle pyramids; the triangle enables opposites to balance and transcend to a new wholeness they couldn't achieve by themselves. A third leg makes a tripod stable, and a third strand of hair allows a braid to knot as one whole. The triangle is the strongest and most stable of shapes and so appears in the constructions of humans and nature. Trinities appear in nature, as worldwide religious symbols, and in spiritual art, which uses the unseen triangular frame to convey this archetypal power.

I would like to share with you these words from Tablet 11 of the Emerald Tablets of Thoth the Atlantan, just to show how words reflect the use of the number three. This example shows how past civilisations worked with the Universal 3:

Three is the mystery, come from the great one,
Hear, and light on thee will dawn.
In the primeval dwell three unities,
Other than these none can exist.
These are the equilibrium, source of creation,
One God, One Truth, One Point of Freedom.
Three come forth from the three of the balance,
All Life, all Good, all Power.
Three are the qualities of God in his light-home
Infinite Power, Infinite Wisdom, and Infinite Love.
Three are the circles (or states) of Existence:
The Circle of Light where dwells nothing but God,
and only God can traverse it,
The Circle of Chaos where all things by nature arise from Death,
The Circle of Awareness where all things spring from Life.
All things animate are of three states of existence,
Chaos or death, liberty in humanity, and felicity of Heaven.

Another man ahead of his time was Pythagoras; he made influential contributions philosophy and religion in the late 6th century BC. He is often revered as a great mathematician and scientist, and is best known for the Pythagorean theorem, which bears his name. But ancient culture in Egypt, and in much earlier times in other parts of the world already new this, as it was passed to them from higher beings and intelligence.

You have heard of the third eye, relating to a part of your brain that is spiritually connected to the universe. Well this is based on you using a part of your brain that can connect to us in Utopia and the universe.

I could go on and on with this subject, but I just wanted to give you a glimpse of how your numbers can affect your world, and

how messages have been left for mankind by the us(
Investigate the meaning of other numbers to help yo)
friends.

If you all sat up and took more notice, read about it and took an interest, there is a lot of evidence in your world, which can trigger more things being revealed. Say in your thoughts every day, and visualise its reality: *"The earth's ancient secrets are revealed to us, we are safe and prepared for this new knowledge."* When you say this, you must have no doubt this will manifest, the mind of mankind is very powerful – so start to use it!

If you join the dots of all the evidence on your earth, you will see that over time, mankind was visited and influenced by off-world civilisations.

I visualise for you learning establishments for all your young to study Spiritualism, and discover first-hand the evidence we have placed before you on these pages. These places could evaluate and decipher the messages and signs left for mankind. How exciting this would be – oh my, mankind would really open up your world if this could happen. You need to create future thinkers who can work beyond the shackles that restrain your mind.

Chapter 4

Your children are your future

Your earth's children are born with the purest of innocence. They come into your world with love and pure openness, and the essence to make your world the best place it can be. Their minds are clear and set at a high frequency of perception. They are very open to the spirit realm world and other dimensions for information. They see things with a clarity that you don't have as adults. As humans grow up you lose the perception you are born with through your fear of the existing world you have created in your minds. Mankind fears a child or grown adult that can perceive things that can threaten the fear beliefs mankind has created. Through fear, the adult will suppress the child until they think like their parents, and feel fear that what they felt and saw was wrong or evil. This fear belief system within most of you is deep in your humanity core, you live with it without realizing you are doing so.

This pureness of love and light your children are born with is a gift to you all. If parents could learn to develop this gift, your world would be the most amazing, peaceful planet with mankind living as one.

This higher frequency way of living in a positive light will draw in the most amazing information and knowledge from the universe. Your technology would develop beyond belief; one of the achievements would be clean energy for a healthy planet, and knowledge to grow food to feed all of mankind in a caring, clean and organic way. You would also learn to communicate telepathically with each other; this is a form of ascension. Remember, a few ancient societies from 10,000 years ago, were influenced by off-world civilizations and learned this way of communication; some of you have this in your DNA, you just need to rekindle the flame and learn to harness this energy with you. With this heightened way of living, you would manage your world as a whole, making sure no one suffered and all lived with shelter, food, and knowledge through learning.

As soon as your children take their first breath, they are influenced by your words, home environment, how you interact with them, what you teach them, the air they breathe and the time you give them.

As mankind has spread out into the world over the centuries, they have developed their own civilisations, religions and societal behaviors. All of these religions are based around off-world visitors and our realm. But each society sees us in different ways and their understanding of what they see is expressed to every child born in these different parts of your world, then the child absorbs and takes on their people's beliefs.

Over the thousands of years, there have been children scattered amongst these societies who see the love and light and break out of the mould, trying to spread the word: *"We are all as one"*. They could have been seen as healers, witches, sorcerers or philosophers, and their gifts developed and were admired by some, and struck fear into the hearts of others. Some of these people were also influenced by other sources such as our realm and alien species; this was because their minds were open to receive great things to help mankind.

If their actions went against the established religions and beliefs, they were often killed or persecuted and their shining light was put out. The numbers of doubters massively outweighed them and they were suppressed or silenced. If you look through your history books, you will find these people in your stories. The story of Jesus will be the one character of your world's history you will all know about, so take time to read this from your bibles, see into the story and see what you gather from it. More recent inspirers for mankind are Martin Luther King, Jr. and Nelson Mandela; they were eventually free thinking religious men who lived to fight for freedom. After his famous music career, John Lennon took the path of light and peace around the world, and was silenced in his prime. These are just a few of mankind's inspirers in your world's history, you must learn from them and never forget them. Read their life stories and be inspired.

How to achieve living as one in the light of love and peace

The minds and bodies of children

It is for us in our realm to write these words, then stand back and guide you all when you allow us to. But I would like to give you some guidance on how to achieve this. A miracle would be a wave of a hand and your world is as one. But as mankind has free will, and centuries of living in the dark need to be unraveled, you need to take this one step at a time. We feel the secret of this is intelligent thinking and creativity, way beyond what you are capable of now.

First of all adults, who have the responsibility of children or are around children in their lives, should start asking them from a young age how they would like to see their world and how they would improve it. This should start from the moment they are born; show them positive pictures, take them to different Mother Earth environments where you live. As they develop and start to communicate with you and the world around them, start to ask their opinion of the world they see. Don't shield them from bad images or the news. Let them see these and ask them how they would help and how humans can stop this happening. For them to change their world they need to know what to change, and if you shield them – how will they know? Yes, we would love you all to live in a pink bubble of love and light, but you have to face the dark corners of your world to know what to change. Take note of their answers as they progress in their childhood; keep their minds open and clear. Do not push old beliefs on your children, allow them to experience the world and make their own conclusions, and then the answers will come.

Part of the journey to help aid your children, is for the adults of your society's to heal themselves. The reason I say this is to teach your children, you need to be at your best high vibration. To teach the purist and best aspect required for future mankind's needs, you have to be cleared yourself, of fear, guilt, negativity and grief. When your children's life teachers are in this high vibration, your children will learn so much more, opening their minds and be inspired by the presence of their teachers and what they are taught. You will also need to learn how to protect your selves, so you see the world's pain but you do not take on the hurt and negative energy in to your own high vibration, this teaching will then pass to your children. Just think of the amazing beings they can be with this new way of thinking and teaching.

Teach children from a young age to meditate

Your children have busy minds that you call a "monkey mind". This is a great term, as their thoughts will swing round their minds like monkeys in the trees, more so when stressed. If you can teach them from an early age to stay still and meditate, this will change their world. Meditation gives your children the freedom from negative effects of stress and allows the mind to be fresh, inspired and relaxed, and helps bring creativity and clarity.

Young children will naturally have a problem focusing for a long period, so when young, just simply lie on the ground with them and ask them to watch the clouds, counting them. This simple technique will slow down a child's mind. The more you do this with them the better they will get at meditating, and they will become more focused. As your children grow, introduce longer and more focused meditation.

As they develop, meditation will help the development of their academic mind, keeping them de-stressed, more focused and inspired, and opening their minds to more of their potential; believe us, they have vast potential that's not being used at the moment. Mankind's way of thinking in education limits children's mind-set, and many are put into special categories; both child and parent are made to think that they cannot achieve beyond a certain level.

Believe me, my friends, change the way you educate your children and my, won't you be surprised at what they can achieve.

Through meditation, children can discover that there is so much more they can achieve in their lives. They will see that some of the stresses in their lives are petty, they will resolve problems that would normally block them, and they will realise that they can be successful beyond their dreams and imaginations.

Ok – the key, then, is for adults to meditate and be trained so they can pass this on. Meditation is starting to be recognised in the western world and in education, and through their religious beliefs, some eastern countries already include it as part of their daily routines.

You find from day to day, my friends, that your minds can drift from time to time, off to a place you don't see. The unknown source is calling you in, just to be and to rest your minds. Sometimes your concentration feels lost, calmness has swept over you, you wonder at the time you have lost and how you have completed your short task without remembering anything. This is a space in time, which you can find through mediation, where you can rest. To rest your mind strengthens your core and our connection to you. While you are in this calm space we meet, my friends, we heal you, download information and set you on the next stage of your path.

The images and messages you see during meditation are part of this download; think of yourself as the hard drive – you will store this information without realising it and your higher self will help trigger the usage of it when the time comes. The more your mind is in this wonderful space the stronger it will become, and you will be able to build your mind's hard drive to connect to the knowledge of the universe – this is our wish for mankind. Find a meditation group to help you learn and develop this skill.

It will be a couple of generations my friends before you can all tap into this knowledge by just a thought, but if you all start now and pass your meditation skills to your children and grandchildren, you will be helping us to achieve this with you.

This will all take time but if you start now, by the time it reaches the third generation from you, the world will be a different place. The reason we say it will take time is that mankind has a lot of bad habits and mental blocks to shift. Slowly, there are more and more light workers who are spreading this message. See it as a wound that has to slowly heal, gaining strength and energy. Then you will all run at your full potential. We can see this; if only all of you could!

Healthy food intake and resources for your children

A healthy diet is key is for the human body to be at its best. It feeds the mind muscle, and you know that when you lack energy and health, you do not function well. Human bodies need to eat more healthily, and take more organic food. We know your world population is huge, and feeding your world is a big challenge, which is something you need to re-evaluate. We understand the vastness of this task, but you could all start in your own space, by growing vegetables at home and clearing wasteland for allotments. Encourage your community to join you in this; some of you need a leader to follow and encourage them – you can be that leader. These small steps will lead to bigger steps for mankind.

You can also be a champion for raising your animal food in a humane way. These animals give their lives to feed you, and they need respect and dignity. Look at the past civilisations, to American Indians and Australian tribes, and how they give thanks when they kill; they simply take what they need from nature and respect it. As you all move into the love and light way of thinking, this will happen.

Look at the way the world is powered. Earth's resources are running low, and we estimate that in another fifty to a hundred years, you will be struggling. You have three power sources, your sun, wind and ocean; this is where your future lies. If every house had solar panels and a wind turbine, you would save the planet's environment, but you need to start now. The people who control your power supplies will not be very amenable to this because of the wealth it brings, but you all have to rise above it; what matters is Mother Earth, and your children's future.

Pollution of your world is out of hand, and Mother Earth is struggling with this; she tries to adapt but the pace of the damage is too fast for her. Again, mankind is afraid of checking the demand on food supplies, energy and world finance. Each one of you asks us for the resources for you to fit solar panels to your homes, and we will help with this. The world powers need to unit in this, to achieve this way of thinking.

We feel sometimes that the only way mankind will ever take stock is for a big natural disaster on Mother Earth, which will happen if you don't stop and look after her. The humans left behind will re-evaluate and live the way we are suggesting, and your planet will recover. She is a living planet and needs healing. I know we have touched on this already, but we need to spell it out. You have so much potential as a world and you do not see it. You are all one and should live that way for your children's sake.

Sit your children down and give them the future choices of earth, I know which they would pick – for humans to live in touch with Mother Earth and for you to reach your full potential in life and minds.

Their whole being

Every child should know safety and love. This is vital to their nurturing, and the development of their full potential. Help the world achieve this. If there were no wars and famine, this would be possible.

In an ideal world all children would be nurtured, loved and living in a holistic, organic, pollution-free environment; this is what we want for you. I hear you ask: *But is it too late? Is the task just too big?* It is not!

You can start with simple things; from an early age, make your child treasure nature. Show them the beauty of butterflies, the family bond of nature's animals, the importance of plants and the vital strength of your oceans. Teach them about your world; don't rely on their teachers, you need to take control of this learning on their life paths. Bring in healthy eating and a holistic life style. Strive to spread the word to friends and family and the world as a whole. You all need to take responsibility for this. If you have fear of being shunned by people close to you because of your new beliefs, rise above this and they will soon follow you.

Teach your children to accept each other and the world they live in

Acceptance of all that is different is something your children must learn – how they look at earth's different races and religions, or how they respond to a child who is handicapped in some way or physically or mentally different.

Your children need to understand the pureness of the souls that live in these children who are classed as different in your societies. Mankind's mind and ego makes them different. What if the handicapped, slow of learning, physically impaired and emotionally scarred children are the norm, and the rest of you the odd ones out? What is normal? This is just a word, my friends. Once children have accepted that others are different and do not ridicule them, the children will become as one in your world and take this into adulthood. Once acceptance is achieved, you have taken a big step forward for the human race. A quote from mankind: *"There's only one race, the Humankind Race, and within it, many different cultures."* It will take a generation or so to clear old societies' thoughts and racism, and this has to start with parenting. Children only learn from their parents and their societies; there is a lot to unravel, my friends. Please, change your mind-set and teach your children these vital lessons.

Spiritualism can be brought into your education systems, to give your children, young teenagers and adults this choice. All religions should be taught for the greater understanding of the mind and mankind, with the spiritualism religion (as it will be called) taught alongside them. Recently there are groups and societies springing up everywhere in your western world, starting to spread the word and bring this spiritualism religion and way of thinking to you and your education systems.

Your whole ethos of life can be in love and light, pureness of heart and greater understanding of others, your true values set before you and your children as a way of life. Part of this is a holistic approach to health and wellbeing; healthy bodies lead to healthy minds, helping you to expand into a higher vibration, all for the good of your children and teachings. See the bigger picture, my friends, it's not hard.

How are we helping you on this path?

It's all very well me going on about what you can do, but you do need our help, and we are working behind the scenes, my friends, to aid you with your children. Some of you will have heard of Star Children. They are being born amongst you to help mankind move forward and evolve. They possess psychic, spiritual and other extra-sensory abilities. These children will bring peace, topple corrupt systems, and shift dimensional consciousness in the years to come.

We have divided them into three categories on your earth to help aid your understanding of them: Indigo, Crystal, and Rainbow. The Star Children have chosen specific parents and grandparents who will help them develop their natural abilities. So if you are a parent of a child you class as different from the norm, your child probably chose you to help them help others in their spiritual path. They have slowly been coming to earth for over a century, but in the last twenty years, there have been a lot more. The increase is because mankind has shifted to accept these children more into their societies and the fifth dimension energy can now filter down more to your third dimension world.

How to recognise an Indigo child: The Indigo children are passionate in their beliefs, whatever they may be, and the strength of their feelings can often be overwhelming for them. These children want to know the truth and want to break down the patterns of traditional thinking. The Indigos have a specific purpose, which is to seek out the truth and change archaic systems of thought on the old energy grid, and usher you into a new world of integrity. They are creating a path and unveiling lies and secrecy to help Crystal Children who will see the world from an elevated platform of spirituality, and a highly evolved viewpoint with complete and unconditional love. A lot of your indigo children will have what are considered to be behavioural problems, which are called Attention Deficit Hyperactivity

Disorder (ADHD) and similar labels. These children will be misunderstood by others not on the love and light path, but remember, you were chosen as a parent because you will understand your child and guide them towards their desired goal. Remember they are here to create a new energetic frequency, and to bring about 'one world' populated by unique, individual, free-thinking people living in the fifth dimension.

Crystal children: They started to appear more in the last twenty-five years. Their main purpose is to take you to the next level in your evolution and reveal to you your inner and higher power. They function as a group consciousness rather than as individuals, and they live by the Law of mankind to be one. They will also be advocates for love and peace on Mother Earth. The first thing you will recognize about Crystal children is their forgiving nature. They are very sensitive, warm and caring. Don't mistake these characteristics as a sign of weakness, as Crystal children are also very powerful. They can be multi-faceted and able to see outside the box, yet must also play and find their way in your three-dimensional world so they do not become isolated and alone. They can tune into the universe, they have high intuition – you will not be able to hide anything from these children, because they are all seeing.

Rainbow children: They are coming amongst you more frequently and they have been building in the last few years. Rainbow children bring joy and harmony to their families. Unlike the Indigo and Crystal children, the Rainbow child is born to smile, which is accompanied by their huge hearts that are full of forgiveness. Rainbow children are psychic and have the ability to read people's feelings. This gift is usually revealed as they grow older. They will become light workers and advocates of our realm. One of their purposes is to complete the final stages of the foundation that the Indigo and Crystal children have made.

With the energy shift, there will now be more and more born to take away your world's pain and help build a new world. I have just written a glimpse of this for you; there are books on your earth about these children, written by light workers; please study them and spread the word amongst your societies. This will help you recognise them and nurture them. But please do not single out these children, they need to grow up in the society they are born into to complete their life's work where they are needed.

Nurturing your young

The other factors we would like you to consider is when we blend with a human physical body, the memories are wiped as we mix with your energy. There are cases when the human physical form can struggle with having this energy with-in them. As they develop, this creates a feeling of loneliness, not belonging thoughts and feelings they will experience that other humans don't have and understand. Some of you will have come across depressed, lonely people, children that seem detached, who seem lost and don't fit in with the 3D world man has created and some might have mental illness.

As well as the human body struggling to take the new soul, other influences behind this connection break down is their environment and bad human influences. We know if every child was nurtured from day one, with carming environment, introduction of meditation and the higher energy of love and light, this will stop this happening on earth. Mankind would become free of illness; detachment disorders and every one would have a place in your society.

A lot of physical illness are triggered from your mental mind state and polluted environment. So again I repeat clean up your world, live holistically, balance mankind and as you lift your vibrations all of this will lift away from mother earth, healed and living in love and light.

So remember my friends your earth children are born with the purest of innocence. They come into your world with love and pure openness, and the essence to make your world the best place it can be. Let go of your ego and pride and change your lives so your children's futures can be the best they can.

Chapter 5

Glimpses of Utopia

Throughout mankind's history there have been glimpses into our beautiful realm Utopia and we have shown our spirit selves to you. These have been at times when you have needed our comfort, love and reassurance, when an Angel appears or you have what you call an afterlife experience and you are allowed to remember it. Or you have started on a spiritual path, which has given you a connection with spirit and glimpses of our realm. The miracles in your books through history show some of these experiences in their tales. We would like to share with you modern day experiences from everyday people living what you would call normal lives. It will surprise you to learn how many of you do have an experience like this, but choose not tell others because you are afraid of being ridiculed. But you know its meaning deep inside and know it was not your imagination.

We felt it is important to share these stories to give hope to others, enlighten mankind and show that your world could be a loving pure experience if mankind allowed it. There is a shift towards the light; you can help this shift by sharing these experiences, so please share your own stories and these printed here, with your friends and families. When you start sharing, you will be surprised how many people will have their own story to tell, which will resonate with you.

True stories from some of your lovely earth people

Mel's story

I want to write and tell you my story in a few words, of how I managed to overcome drug abuse, mental abuse and self-harm, by discovering spirit and the path of love and light.

From the fear of real life and rejection

The path of darkness is the easy option. Taking the path of love, trust and strength is the hardest of them all. The road of darkness is so easy to follow because of all the substances that suppress and block your love and strength from within.

The path of the light is hard to start because there is no help apart from your trust and belief in something not completely found at first. But when you do, the love and light and strength is bigger than you ever could imagine.

The dark road is so dark and unhappy that you think twice before entering it again, and you know the light will bring you back if you ask.

Thank god I found the light that brought me through the dark, endless pain. Now there is light, love, trust, happiness and most of all, faith in myself.

I would like to dedicate this to the spirit world and Heaven Sent, my newfound family.

Love and light blessed be.

I have to sing the praises of Mel for telling you her story. When humans do drugs or are abused, it takes great strength to rise up, bury your mind's demons and pick yourself up out of darkness and into the light. Her experiences will one day help others, as this is her path. She is now a light worker; great things lie ahead for her and for those humans that become part of her journey.

Joanne's Story

I've been working with the spirit world for 7 years and it has completely changed my Life. Before I knew about the spirit world I was afraid of dying, and wondered what happens when you die. But now I have no fear of dying, as I know it's only a change of world.

As a child I experienced a sense of someone sitting on my bed, and I always wondered what that was, but I now know why I felt that. I believe that it was a sign that I had gifts of spirit, but was too young to know at that time.

I've had visits from my loved ones in my dreams. I've spoken to them and they speak back, it's a wonderful experience and feels as if you're in a different world — in their world for that short time.

I have heard spirit call out to me and they have also shown me future events before they happen, which do happen a while later.

Hope you enjoy my story.

Jo's story is from a light worker; she has been working with us for a while now, she trusts all she feels and experiences with the Spirit world, she has no fear and enjoys her life on earth working with us. The special place Jo has achieved is where all mankind can be. Jo is a pure soul to this day, her thoughts always of love and light. Her journey in life has not been easy, my friends, but she knows she is loved and cherished by spirit, and this has helped her lift into the love and light vibration.

Teuila's story

I have always believed in angels and went through a phase where I collected every angel-like thing in sight — whether it was jewellery, statues, soft toys or whatever. And doves. Oh boy, I loved doves!

It really got me through my depression. There was one episode that really struck me as, *"Oh my goodness! They really do exist!"* I had gone through severe depression, and one night it got to the point of being like a maniac and I just wanted to end the pain. I'm a religious sleeper (fall asleep 10 pm every night, phone goes on silent, friends know how useless it is to contact me etc). But that night I wasn't. I was so close to the edge, and at 2 am, a friend (who to this day claims he was just feeling like he really needed to call) called for no reason other than to ask if I was ok, talked me through everything, and convinced me to go to the ER. That was my first encounter – why on earth would he call at that time, knowing I never answer my phone anyway? And he felt he was told something was wrong.

The second - In hospital, the depression manifested as something sinister in my dreams. I remember one night lucidly dreaming that I was trying to sleep. All of a sudden I could hear heavy breathing and laughing and a raspy voice saying, *"You're mine."* I remember freaking out and thinking, *"Please God, please angels..."* The shadowy thing manifested at the end of my bed and I remember panicking more and more until all of a sudden, this white light shot from above my head and chased the thing off.

The third - Two years later, another downturn of depression hit. The same thing happened – a friend, who had no idea how close I was to ending it all, called at what would've been my last breath... because she just 'felt like calling'.

There have been many more encounters, but I think these three are the most powerful and significant for me. They pulled me from my darkest hours... as they do for everyone. I pray that people who feel they are in that dark place as well, will read these encounters and that my story gives them hope. Even if just a little...

Blessings and thank you for the opportunity to share my story.

Teuila's story is an example of her inner self-crying out for help and her guides and angels listening and sending it to her. Her mind was in a dark place, but her soul and higher self knew it was not her time to come home; so she received the help she needed, the love and reassurance; this has then helped her move forward on her journey on earth towards the love and light of spirit way of thinking, helping to take away the pain of her depression.

Gemma's Story

Many years ago when my son (who has Asperger's) was about four, we were in his grandma's car and all of a sudden he said he had seen an Angel – we had never discussed angels etc with him. I asked if it was an old lady, because I was thinking it might have been my Nan. He said she was a beautiful woman ... and then he said he had seen the spirit of a boy in his room too ... he seemed to know the difference. It was only the one time it happened, and he never said he had seen them again. He wasn't worried or frightened; he's a very gentle soul. My other son used to see auras when he was younger, but not any more; it's a shame they have to grow up and these gifts don't always stay.

Gemma's story reflects the indigo child of pure spirit and knowing, in your world. A lot of the indigo children are autistic, have Aspergers and other learning difficulties that might make others shun them. They are pure of soul and others will learn from them on their life's journey. Is it not interesting that she said her son grew out of this psychic ability? With the right nurturing, your children can retain this gift and excel.

Anna's Story

I found my angels about twenty years ago; they came into my life after I was separated. They have been the most amazing beings to me; there are so many things they have done for me. They always find parking spaces for me; even my grandchildren call on them to find us one. There is one story that I have to tell. It was when I was having a bad day. I was a little short of money, and they had always made sure there was enough to eat and pay my bills. But I was thinking I would love something new for myself. I went to my wardrobe and was putting some washing away; when I opened my dress, 20 euro just flew out from nowhere! No way, it was there because it flew out and landed at my feet, it was their way of giving me a treat. x

Anna's story reflects the simple help we can give in your day-to-day lives if you ask us for it. We are always waiting. You are all searching from within for the spiritual path. These simple gestures from us help guide you towards it, if you are open to this.

Tamaryn's story

My Gran and I were extremely close. Although I was only seven at the time of her death, I have always felt her presence around me. She used to fetch me from primary school often; even if it rained, she would walk to the school in her little heels and umbrella to fetch me. We had a strong bond like no other. Granny got sick and moved into our house for a couple of weeks, and suddenly had a heart attack and was taken from us. Because of my unexplainable great love for her, I slept in the bed where granny laid before she passed on. One night I awoke, and as I opened my eyes, a white shadow came in through the bedroom door. It came right up to the side of my bed, and I couldn't believe my eyes. It was Granny kneeling in a praying position, I could recognise her face, and had this overwhelming sense of calm over me. It was this visit that has made me such a spiritual being. And I thank God.

A lot of your light worker journeys will start witnessing a loved one in spirit; they are there offering you love and protection, so there is no need to fear. This was a sign Tamaryn received; she recognised the significance of it, which led her on her spiritual path to trust in us. These signs are planned before you come to earth; we set them in place and we hope you will recognise them and that your free will set you on the right path. This is what we always hope for. If at first we don't succeed, we try again if this is in your life plan.

Nicole's story

When I was 15 I felt so alone. The pain of this was so unbearable that I just wanted to end it all; I tried on many occasions earlier in life, but there was one particular time that was serious and I was hospitalised. My mother was desperate to get me to communicate, and with the help of one of her friends I was introduced to a beautiful soul named Chrissie. This lady very tenderly introduced me to myself, helped me to understand how I functioned as a human being, and then introduced me to the concept of Angels. With gentle care, I became stronger within myself, my confidence grew and then I learned about the importance of self-love. My faith in love, spirit and the angels grew and one day while at school, I was walking across the schoolyard; there was not a student in sight and I asked my angel this question: If you are real then prove it to me now. I want to feel you. I need to know you exist! I walked a couple of steps further then my right hand was embraced with the most loving touch. A most amazing warm flow of love engulfed my arm and spread to the rest of my body. My heart swelled with joy and I cried. I cried at the love I couldn't see but could only feel. I walked hand in hand across that schoolyard, knowing I would never be alone again.

Nicole's story is a wonderful example of being touched by an earth angel when in need; many of your healers on earth come in many forms amongst you. This experience then opened up her heart to receive us and she now walks on a path of light and love. Her mind experienced the dark, negative world that mankind creates for a while, then she was touched by her guardian angel. When you first see the light it is awesome, and a wonderful feeling to be lifted into, all mankind could have this if you opened your hearts. She will go on to tell her story to others to lift their hearts, as part of her life's journey.

Erja's Story

I have two stories. I feel in hindsight that there were Angels in disguise that came down to help me in each situation.

In 1980, I had started studying law at university and was travelling on a bus home one fine day during the week. I sat next to an older woman, well put together, long hair tied up and average weight; being a nice person, I started a conversation with her. As it was a fair ride on the bus of at least thirty minutes, the conversation progressed well. I felt safe with her and she was so positive in everything she said. I do remember thinking, I thought all older people just talked about their ailments and negative things or just about themselves. She wasn't like that. I remember thinking, I want to be just like her when I'm older, which I am now, and I do not speak about my ailments and I try to be as positive as I can. This woman was an Angel sent down in physical form to show me what my future could be like, and it is like that. I still remember that woman in a loving way and wish I could tell her how appreciative I am for all her efforts in 1980.

Fast-forwarding to 1986, I was still married to my first husband and had two children, aged three and just under two years of age.

One day – I'm not sure which month it was – I was driving through the outskirts of the city of Brisbane, and I had the children in the car with me. I slowed to a stop near a post office; in those days it was a main thoroughfare, but not as busy as these days. When I came out of the post office, I noticed a lady wearing an old-fashioned nursing or nanny outfit with a long dress and a nursing hat, and it looked like something out of the last century. She was helping an older gentleman who was blind into the front seat of my car. Cars back then didn't self-lock so my door was open and I made no effort to stop her. I was shocked to say the least. She spoke to me and asked me to take the gentleman to Edward Street, a main road in the city not far from where I was. Being a helpful person, of course I agreed. I remember thinking that my children were totally silent and I don't remember what we spoke about. However, I felt wonderful, and when he left, I was so happy, with a peace I can't describe.

I told everyone in the family about my experience, and I did voice my feeling that he was an Angel. Everyone was negative about my comments. Now I know both those people were Angels in physical form, sent to help me and make me feel loved. The feeling from that day still fills me with joy and love and I know it was Spirit, as I have red cheeks from doing this email about them. That's always a sign Spirit is with me ....

Fast forwarding again to 25th May 2015 ... After learning to trust, I can now receive Angel messages, or automatic writing, and they have given me the confidence that working in Spirit is soooo possible and enriching...

Blessings Erja

Oh how I love this story of Erja's progression, towards her recognition of the pure love we can give. Through her events in her life she recognised angel intervention, this is when her light blub went on, a spark of the divine. A lot of you on the light worker journey will resonate with this, when you look back at times in your life, you now know we were there helping guiding your inner soul that was asking for help.

Catherine's story

I can say with confidence that I felt angels around me during my first Reiki session. It was very clear and obvious that I was surrounded and touched by them. I was warm and comforted, beautiful, safe and calm.

These few simple lines show how the Reiki path can attune you to connect to us in our realm and guide you on your life's path. Many light workers start their journey towards love and light through the Reiki path.

Jeanne's story

I feel my story really began over thirty-six years ago when we moved into our house. Built in 1890 with coach horse stables at the back. It was in a poor state of decay, but we had just got married & loved it.

However when we started to restore it, the spiritual activity began. We both knew nothing about this sort of thing, but as a child I did have a sense of spirit, but my parents did not. This is a whole story in itself, but I just want to share how I feel the angels have led me to the work I'm doing now.

One day I experienced a vision seeing a creature I could not explain by an oak tree. The best way I can describe the creature is he was small stature, like a fairy being of some kind, dressed in a bright green cloak with a crocked staff. I felt although I could not clearly see his face, that he was ancient & wise. I believe I saw some kind elf!!!! After this we decided to go to Glastonbury to see if I could find something to help me understand what I had seen. We had a lovely holiday home at the time, which was not far from Glastonbury. The only problem was that in all the time we had been in Somerset, staying at our holiday home every year for some 25 years, I just could not spend a day in Glastonbury town, because every time I got out of the car, I just could not stand up at all! It was so odd. I seemed to sense all the energy of the place. But on the next day after my vision I was totally fine once out in the main high street, and have been ever since!

Once I was back at home I looked in books etc to see if I could find anything that resembled what I had seen by the oak tree. I had just found a magazine at the time called Soul & Spirit; I sent an email to the editor about my encounter. I described the creature that it seemed to mimic me, and the colours I saw.

To my surprise my answer was published in the next month's issue....

My answer I received was as follows...

JENNY SAYS, *"This was not a trick of the light. The clue is in the mimicking. Mirror angels are a reflection of the state of your soul, and this is what this vision was showing you. The green represents the healing you are so good at. The small stature of being reflects that after your illness, you have yet to grow back to your full power. Your angel has shown me the same figure, as you can see with shades of green & gold too, which in time means you will reach your potential.*

The fact that the figure wouldn't follow your path means there will be a divergence from what you currently see as the only way to your destiny, and the true reason for you being here. The message is to stay open, be ready, watch for further signs, and they will come, be flexible and follow your angel's directions".

It took me a while to process this reply, but then it all started to happen.

Trained many years ago as an SNU healer with the spiritualist church, I was all happy and comfortable in my sanctuary. But then I started to receive parts of trees for the clients during the sessions. Not saying anything at the time, I decided to buy a book called The Healing Power of Trees by Jacqueline Memory Paterson. To my amazement, every tree part I had received matched the clients' complaints!

I have since learned that this is the essence of nature being given to me for the healing. I knew nothing about the Elementals, but I somehow felt I was being guided to learn & work with their powers. I bought an angel bible and read on pages 62 & 63 about these energies. We started to be woken up in the night with very bright lights coming from the healing room; this still happens every now and again, especially when another change happens to me with my development. An experienced medium came to visit me and said she could feel the angels & fairies all around the house.

I now remember that before I even started to train as a healer, the events from the house that led me to the church for help, were caused by what I now understand to be poltergeist activity. I've learned how to pray & work with my guides and guardian angel, and how to respect the spirit world. I now teaching development circles, and I know that it is not a game.

I was about twenty-six when things stopped in the house, and I started to see spirit guides, and so this gave me an interest to sit and develop further. Now I have linked this next experience to the one I had in 2009.

On returning home from picking our son up from school, I entered his bedroom to find a whole room full of dried leaves. The window was shut; we have no trees in our garden! I have since learned that they were the dried leaves from an alder tree. I live near Aldershot, where they cut down forests of alder trees to build for the army back in the 1800s.

Our house was built by the army at the same time, on ancient woodland. When I looked in my tree book, I found to my amazement that alder trees have been slept on for the relief of rheumatism, by filling cushions, pillows & duvets - even today. My husband had just been diagnosed with rheumatism in his hips & spine ... was this a sign of what I would be working with now, much later on in my life??? Alder trees are linked to the element of water.

Every time we visited our holiday home in Somerset, we felt so blessed & lucky to have it. It was a very rugged and remote place, with a large natural waterfall flowing down onto the beach. The element of water arrived, as you can see from sea energy healing packs on Google. My journey from this continues, but I also did not know, after all the pictures came of the mermaids, that there is a legend about mermaids at the bottom of the waterfall.

Also strange to me at the time, before I started to develop as a medium, was a grey lady who came to me many times, whenever we stayed in Somerset. I looked in all the graveyards trying to find her. I had no name, but she kept leading me to a special place by the waterfall. Years later, when I found a book written by a local historian, and was reading about the legend of the mermaids, I found the story of the Grey Lady on the next page. She has been reported for many years around the area, and in the great St Audrey's house, where she was often seen tucking the girls up in bed at night – as the house was a girls' school in the 1950s.

I've since gone on to study Mantic Arts, with which I hope to continue further.

My journey continues....

Much light in all that you do with your wonderful work.
Jeanne & the Mer-people & Fairy Whispers. xx

This story really shows her connection with the elementals; I know she has worked with them before this life. This story shows how wonderful it is when they crop up on your path and then it's up to you to resonate with the signs and choose your path.

Rusty's story

Around eight or nine years ago, I was invited to a Mind Body and Spirit Event. To be honest, at the time I was a bit low and couldn't find a way of pulling myself out of it. So I didn't really want to go and I really didn't want to be there. After tootling round some stalls, we went to an Angel talk.

There were around 200 people in the room, and at the front was the lady doing the talk. It was a wonderful talk and included a meditation introducing us to Archangel Michael, who was helping us heal. He was cutting the ethereal chords draining us of negative energy and anything that was holding us back. Archangel Michael rode into my meditation on a huge horse, dressed in blue, looking like the actor in Zorro! Wielding a huge shiny sword and a very big shiny shield, it was as if the chords were being cut.... by a hedge trimmer! I can honestly say, the weight of the world was being lifted off my shoulders. As more and more were cut, the tears started...and I couldn't stop. I sobbed and I sobbed and I sobbed. I could not stop it, I didn't want to, I couldn't help it and I didn't care. It was wonderful!!! At one point, I had to open my eyes and I could still see Archangel Michael stood in front of me

We left the room and went outside, as I really did need air. I took my boots off and stood on the grass and cried some more... but none of this was out of sadness. It was totally liberating. Once I'd composed myself and reapplied my mascara... I literally floated round for the rest of the day.

On another occasion, the Archangels introduced themselves to me - I was hit with a bright blue flash and yellow strike/stripe as Archangel Michael blasted in at full force. It wasn't alarming but he was on a mission, strong and powerful and flashing his sword about me. It was a kind of hi and bye too, as he'd introduced himself before and wanted me to know he was still a force of power.

Archangel Jophiel arrived on a skateboard, looking like a cherub. Quite a cheeky cherub he was too, whizzing around me, which really made me smile and lifted my spirits. That's one way of being illuminating and wise!

Archangel Gabriel was the most brilliant and purest form imaginable. I can't even put into words what I saw, but it was huge, bright, perfect and amazing.

Archangel Raphael had the softest touch and the waves of healing flowing over and through me were amazing.

Archangel Uriel seemed to open my eyes at this point, not literally, but I felt them open, as if I was seeing the truth for the first time, and saw gold rods of light. During all this, even more waves of healing were washing all over and through me, flowing from the top of my head to the bottom of my feet. I was so in awe at this point that some of it is a bit of a blur. But I saw pictures of a very small girl with light hair, followed by someone rather lovely saying my name. This person was either a lady with long grey hair or a Native American Indian with long grey hair. But I couldn't make it out, or tell if it was male or female. (I now know him as my other Guardian Angel since birth, he's since been back and is a Native American Indian; the little girl was me).

Then waves of pure love flowed, followed by a lot of light, all different colours, all bright and beautiful, turned into flowers and petals, and I felt freedom and at peace. I now recognise him as Archangel Zadkiel, and I was beaming inside from ear to ear.

A wonderful experience ... but I was one Archangel missing. What happened? Did I do something wrong? Why didn't he show up? That night I went to bed... and then I felt what I can only describe as a total surprise and total blissfulness. As I closed my eyes and was drifting off - Archangel Chamuel arrived!!! He'd waited, and clearly needed more time with me … and this huge, pure pink cloud mist or mystical form surrounded me, gently took away my heart, cleaned it, purified it and replaced it with a lighter and more loving one. Then these huge wings of total pink love and purity surrounded and hugged me and I fell asleep in these wings.

To this day, I can't properly describe that night; words fail me, but the feelings and experience stays with me all the time. I see flashes of blue all over the place when Archangel Michael is with me and he sits on my car bonnet with his sword charging forward! Jaguar cars eat your heart out; you have a cat on the front. Here we have Archangels! He kicks me up the ass to motivate me. Archangel Jophiel still makes me laugh, lightens my spirit and makes me see the beauty in everything. When I'm doing a Reiki treatment, I know Archangel Raphael is with me. I can feel the power of his healing and more often than not, he stands opposite me. He's a green mist that surrounds me, too.

To date, this is how I still see and feel the Archangels and my Guardian Angels. When I feel my Female Guardian Angel I feel very tingly and soft and gentle warmth – she sends tingles from my lips down my neck. And I feel very comforted and protected at the same time. Just recently they opened an email at work I was going to leave until later… this gave me information that I'd actually made a big mistake. But it also gave me the opportunity and time I needed to put it right!!

I say good morning to my Angels & Guides every day, to help strengthen my connection; and at night, I thank them for always being with me. After the Angel talk I also now realise why I buy things in threes and arrange things in threes - that's my Angels!!! Because there are three levels or three spheres in each level, and each of these contains three levels – they'd been beside me all the time and everywhere! And that's why I know I'm on the right path, teaching Reiki, teaching meditation and now telling you about the Archangels.

But this enlightenment has made me look back at events when I know the angels helped me. Here are a few: I'd asked my friend if I could borrow her Oyster card for another friend, as we were off to London and it's easier to use a card to get around. I'd also mentioned it was a flying visit and I couldn't hang around as it was my only night off. So I went round after work to pick it up. Instead of having it ready for me, she had to hunt high and low for it, as it wasn't in the place where she'd always kept it. At the time I was really frustrated about it. I was tired and all I wanted to do was grab a bottle of wine from the corner shop, go home, have a bath, put my PJs on and snuggle up with the cats. This delay actually saved me. My Angels clearly wanted me to avoid something... I did eventually leave my friend's half an hour later, and go to my local corner shop.

As I walked in, there was a queue at the counter, which at the time I did find odd. I picked up some wine and joined the queue. Then I was informed it wasn't a queue, they were all there to help. Fifteen minutes before I walked in, the owner had been held up at gun point and told to hand over the money from the till. If my friend hadn't held me up, I'd have walked into the shop as the robbery was taking place. I wasn't meant to be there, to foil the robbery, help or assist in any way, because the Angels had brought in someone else - a brave gentleman, who did walk in, tackled the robber and then had to chase him down the street. With help from the police, the robber was arrested. Just how blooming lucky was I? When I got home, I thanked my Angels and phoned my friend to thank her for holding me up, that the Oyster card wasn't where it should be and that my Angels knew best. This isn't the first time either. I have been in situations regarding three other robberies for different reasons.

There was one when I was on holiday. I woke up desperate for the bathroom, all I had to do was roll over, but I remember the distinct feeling that I was put back to sleep. I still can't describe what happened, but I was literally stopped in mid-flow of getting out of bed. Our room had been robbed – that's what had woken me; but probably due to the fact I wasn't wearing pyjamas and it was a dangerous situation, the Angels protected us and made me hang on for the bathroom until morning.

After landing at the airport from the same holiday, we went back to my house and dropped my case off. Then we decided to go to the pub for our evening meal. One of the party mentioned they had a headache. I knew they had some medication in their case. I was going to get it, but I was talked out of it. This is not something that usually happens, and then we got distracted. On returning to the car, it had been broken into and the suitcases had been taken. Later, they were found by the police; they had been ransacked, and all money, jewellery and duty free taken. The question is, why did we go to mine first, and drop off my case, instead of going straight to the pub?

And back in my pub days, I witnessed a robbery happening across the road from the pub I was running. Later, I was told the robbers were wanted by the police for a lot of reasons and other criminal activity, but because of their reputation, no one would testify against them. However, I would. Funnily enough, when I went to testify, I wasn't called into court. The fact I was there and willing to testify was enough for a guilty plea. I just sat chatting to the police, drinking coffee and eating cake under armed guard! These are a few of my bigger examples of how the Angels have helped me, some of which happened before I'd actually met the Angels or knew details about them, as I do now. Love and Angel blessings x x x x x

Rusty has had an amazing, awesome enlightenment experience with her Angels, being opened up at a moment in her life when she was in a place of darkness. She also then recognised when she had been guided and helped along her path by her guides and angels, being kept safe for this amazing event in her life. Through this experience she now teaches and passes on her experiences to others, helping to bring more of you to the love and light so the angels and guides can help and move your life journeys on to their next stage of development on earth.

Avril's story

I was a "young" thirteen years old when my dog, a poodle, was dying. My mother, who never let me miss school unless I was ill, said I could stay at home, BUT I had this inner urge to go to school, as I wanted to ask the Sisters at the Convent to pray for him, which I did.

However, instead of getting peace of mind, I was shocked and heartbroken when a Sister said they couldn't pray for my dog, as *"dogs have no souls"!* When I returned home at lunchtime (my mother had written me a note), sadly my dog had passed and been taken away. My grief was now doubled and I remember crying and just staring out of a window to the sky.

What happened next was not in my imagination. I was with my mother and two sisters who also witnessed the following, ALL portrayed in cloud formations. Firstly, a cloud took the shape of a poodle's head ... then the head became smaller, peering out of what I can only describe as a "Cinderella" type carriage. More clouds joined to form four or six horses, which attached to the carriage. Then there appeared a long and winding path that the carriage and horses travelled up, all getting smaller with distance. At the top of the path was a fairytale-type castle and the carriage and horses seemed to go through the castle gates. The cloud formations then dispersed. I genuinely believe Spirit was letting me and my family know that our dog HAD gone to a heavenly place and I am as grateful today as I was at the time, for the peace it gave.

This story reflects the way we can send you signs to help comfort and reassure you, such as cloud shapes and rainbows, which are our favorites. We also love robins, butterflies, feathers and coins to show we and your passed loved ones have been around you. But unless you believe in us, these signs are wasted, as you do not see them as a message and our sign of love. I would also like to add, my friends, that your animals do have souls and come back home to us safe and sound.

Tony's story

"I believe in Angels" ... so the ABBA song goes and lots of other songs of course refer to Angels.

Well I have a story to tell about my encounter one night back in January 1991 where I believe my life was saved not once, but twice in one evening, with the intervention of my Guardian Angel.

In 1991, after three years of working for the Foreign and Commonwealth Office, I was leaving my home in Northampton to come and work back in St. Anne's, Lancashire, for a large Government IT Agency. I had been using the car to transport stuff on Sunday nights as I travelled back. I had so much stuff I asked if anyone had a little trailer I could borrow. Fortunately, a colleague had one lying around and so I borrowed it. One particular Sunday in January, I loaded up the little trailer for the first time, checked the tyres' condition, pressures, brakes etc. and all seemed good. It was winter and it was raining heavily as I set off around 6pm. The trailer pulled well and the journey was trouble free as I stayed at a steady 50mph. It was a dark, cold night, and the roads were busy with lorries, spray and strong winds.

I passed the M6 Hilton Park Services in good time, but a few miles later, I felt the car sway heavily from side to side and then suddenly, the car lifted itself up from the slow lane, turned itself around and put me in the fast lane of the M6 ... facing all three lanes of oncoming traffic. All I could see were three sets of headlights streaming towards me in the spray. Instinctively, I just put my foot down on the accelerator, turned the wheels fully clockwise and headed towards the lights, trying to 'U' turn the car towards the hard shoulder. At that moment, a very calm peace came over me and the car just crossed – seemed to be gliding to be honest – in the paths of all the oncoming lorries and cars, then settled itself on the hard shoulder. I just sat there, wondering what on earth had just happened. My heart was racing and all I could do was wonder how I survived that. The tyre on the off side of the trailer had just burst and shredded, causing the trailer to swing.

Well, after calling breakdown services, a truck took me to their garage. It would be about 10.30pm by now. They put a new tyre on, as there was no spare. I left the garage around 11.30pm to get back onto the M6 and continue my journey to St. Anne's.

I rejoined the motorway and was merrily but cautiously sticking to a slow speed again. It was still raining heavily, with lorries, noise and spray everywhere. I was reflecting on what had happened earlier. Unbelievably, the car again started to sway heavily from side to side, in exactly the same fashion as before. Again, the car threw itself onto the fast lane and again I was facing all three lanes of the motorway – and there were the same three sets of lights facing me through the spray. Again, I did exactly the same and locked the steering wheel right, selected first gear and put my foot down to do another 'U' turn and get onto the hard shoulder. Amazingly, that same calm and peaceful moment came over me again and the car took itself onto the hard shoulder.

The other wheel on the nearside just fell off and went bouncing off into the darkness, never to be seen again. The breakdown driver could not believe it and took the trailer to his garage. I then journeyed home. He brought the trailer to me the following day with all the stuff intact. I believe my life was saved that night by a strong presence of my Guardian Angel/s. The odds of what happened and also surviving unscathed… I don't know… but I can imagine they would be pretty high.

As I mentioned earlier in the book, we can intervene on your path to keep you safe. You have a planned path, but as with all of the best-set plans, things can crop up that can threaten your life or someone else's. We might intervene because your actions will affect someone else's path and vice-versa. This can also be a trigger for you to see the love and light path and start on the light worker's journey. Your strength of mind and free will then decide what path to take. A lot of people might experience a lot of our interventions and never see them, others stand back and see the door opening and the light shines in.

Rachel's story

I would like to tell you about my guide. My Guide is a lovely woman named Michelle. I will not go into details about her life and where she is from, because that is a book in itself. Michelle speaks from a place of love and she is full of love. The most common theme she has in her messages for me and the messages for others above all else is LOVE. Speak in a place of love; come from a place of love. Show love, be love, be kind, show kindness. She says mankind as a whole is lacking compassion and empathy for others. She says humans are quick to turn around and get their vengeance on others if things do not go the way they want them to. She says that we have forgotten where we come from and what we are put here to do, because our true feelings of love are replaced with ego-based human emotions such as hate, anger and jealousy, and when we replace our true feelings with human emotions, it takes up room in our heart for compassion and empathy. She says as hard a lesson as this is, we must give up our negative emotions (hurt, anger, jealousy, etc) and remember the true place that we come from, which is LOVE. This is the common theme that she speaks about.

I love this simple extract from Rachel's journey. You all have guides trying to tell you this message of love and guidance, open up and listen, my friends.

Deborah's story

I believe I was born psychic with mediumship. I know today that I was meant to be on this path and that 'things would keep happening' until I accepted the inevitable.

My earliest childhood memory involved a spirit in the home. Growing up, I would sometimes see, or mostly hear and feel spirits around me. I knew deep down that what I was picking up or seeing was different to what others might have experienced.

For years I hid from it and was scared. However, two distinct things happened that made me question 1) My purpose here on earth and 2) What life is all about.

I was driving to work like a crazy person with my foot down, late as ever, on a country road at 6:50am. I had to be at work for 7am. It was winter, dark and the roads were sheer black ice. I'd come to a small T-junction, stopped briefly, and was about to accelerate again when a homeless lady (I can still see her now) came out of nowhere and walked slowly across the road. I had my full beam on, yet she looked right at me. She didn't wave; she just calmly and slowly walked across the road, staring at me. She didn't seem to have trousers on, she had a long grey coat, just past the hip, and it was freezing. I knew I had to stop; I knew also it was probably a warning. I never saw her again on that stretch of road. Today, I know she was a guardian angel.

Again, in a similar situation, I was driving with my outlaws (in laws!) in the back and my ex-husband next to me. We were going down steep hairpin bends on a beautiful day. I could see a well-dressed sixty-year-old man through the high pine trees. He stood there, in the middle of nowhere, staring at us. I asked the others if they could see him and they could. Same as before, he didn't take his eyes off me or the others in the car, even as we drove past. The others did not think it odd that he was there in the middle of nowhere. Maybe sixty seconds later, I had no brakes on the car. It was like pushing down on lead. I was going very fast, but used the gears to slow down a little more. We luckily came across a garage quickly. A pin-type thing that keeps two pipes together had come off, causing the brakes to fail. Sorry, I have zero knowledge of cars so cannot explain any better.

And finally, the third situation that slapped me in the face, which could not be ignored, was when I was driving my apprentice home after a workshop. I was heading back home; it was dark, on a busy road, when all of a sudden the light inside the car came on. My immediate thought was that my apprentice hadn't shut the passenger door properly. I turned off the light, looked back at the road, and a German Shepherd dog ran across the road in front of my car. So by now, I had registered that there were Angels, guardians and warnings ...

Last year I suffered a breakdown, and it wasn't the first time. They usually lasted about a week at a time. I had already started on my spiritual journey some years before, but I believe that unless I'd gotten the hint, changed my life and got back on track, it would have kept on and on. I worked 60-hour weeks and was very materialistic. I have since embraced what I feel is my true calling, cut my working hours, have more balance in my life and am happier than I've been in years. When I speak to my spirit guides, they tell me they are thrilled. Interestingly, though, whenever things were going well, there wasn't as much activity compared to when things were going wrong. I could list endless accounts, but I'm aware I've rambled on already. x

Deborah's journey is that of a lady who has the psychic abilities strong in her, but her lifestyle was stopping her progressing and seeing the signs. Sometimes it takes a jolt to see the wake-up call. You think you are happy

or your ego says you are, but once you see the love and light path, you start to balance your life and find true happiness.

Sue's story

I first met my Spirit Guardian Angel two and a half years ago. I had been through a rough patch in my life and had gone away to York with a friend of mine to try and cheer myself up. Whilst I was there I we visited a local antique shop. I'd told my friend that I would love to buy something there and that I fancied buying a ring. I had my finger measured and found I was an N1/2. A blooming odd size I thought. I didn't for one moment expect to find any rings of that size at all! As I was looking I came across a beautiful ruby cluster ring. *"I like that one"*, I said to my friend, *"but I bet it's not my size!"* Well it actually was. It was a lot of money and I didn't really think I could warrant spending so much (it was £249) and I had never spent that much money on myself. However, I did have a little savings. My friend can be quite persuasive and on a whim I thought sod it, I'm going to have it, and so I did. It made me sweat for a little bit I can tell you, but I loved it and from the moment I put it on I knew it was meant for me.

Back at home, I was still feeling a bit concerned about the cost, so I sold my engagement and wedding ring to recoup a little of the money (unfortunately I wasn't going to need them anymore). While I was in the shop, I asked the jeweller if she could look at the new ring I'd bought, as I was wearing it. You wonder sometimes if you've paid over the odds in these antique shops. To my surprise, she said it was worth almost £500 and that it was Victorian, and that it was in excellent condition. Wow! I was very surprised.

I've always been very sensitive to spirit, especially feeling their presence but also seeing them, which I was not very keen on, and over the last few years leading up to this time, I had pushed them away. However, I used to visit a wonderful beauty salon, where the staff were all very spiritual and all into mediumship and all aspects of this area, and I found myself being compelled and fascinated by the whole thing. This was leading me onto a new path, but one that I was destined to take. I had become part of a circle, but I felt uneasy with it all.

They were all developing their skills and I didn't feel confident enough. I really don't like giving readings (although I find myself giving them naturally) and I struggled with prescriptive meditation. I couldn't envisage anything while they were walking through it. I didn't want to give up and so I tried all sorts of things to help me. (To be honest, it's only in the past six months that I have managed to understand my own meditation needs, and that's working out just fine.) One particular day whilst I was meditating and holding the ring, I heard as clear as day the word "Love". I had the image of a young lady who was very much in love. That was a very nice feeling.

One of the ladies at the salon did psychometry and said she would like to look at my ring, and so while I was in the salon she took it, held it and as she did so, I had an image of a young lady riding sidesaddle on a horse, looking very splendid. It was then that my friend who was holding the ring said this lady would have been affluent, and that's when I knew that I was seeing the same young woman. I then felt that at least I wasn't making it all up in my head.

At the time, I wanted to really progress and I was thirsty for anything that would connect me to spirit. I was looking at angel cards, dowsing, going to circle and going to evenings of clairvoyance. I was probably trying to run before I could walk, but that's me all over.

During my dowsing, which taught me all sorts of lessons, some which were harsh but needed, I asked about the ring. I was using a dowsing chart, which I really liked, and I got the name

Elsie, and then as it progressed further words started to come. The pendulum was now beginning to swing, and as momentum gathered it became apparent that the ring had indeed belonged to Elsie. I started to ask all sorts of questions and she said she was going to help and guide me along with another spirit, who was my ex husbands grandfather, Ted. I hadn't known him but we had lived in his home for fourteen years and on a couple of occasions I had seen him around the house. There would also be another spirit called Zies. I searched for that name and couldn't find it anywhere, but it has come up many times since and I know now that I have seen him when I was a child and that he was the first spirit guide I had seen.

Things seemed to be going well and I started to hear voices, and would sit quietly and try to hear more. Elsie was working very hard to try to get me to understand her and I'm sure she was frustrated on many occasions. I know she sometimes gets exasperated with me even now, and I can hear her as plain as day.

It was about four months later that I thought about doing my Reiki level 1; a friend suggested that it might help me.

I booked my course and had a great couple of days. Elsie had said it was my path to be a light worker and to help heal others. Little did I know the impact that being opened up would have on my life. My course was on the Tuesday and Wednesday, and on the Friday I went to circle along with my Reiki master. It was not a nice experience for me that evening. The meditation was led by one of the group and as always we closed our eyes, but something for me felt wrong. I could feel a very strong energy pushing against my head and I had never felt like that before. Elsie told me not to be scared but to open my eyes. I did, but the person leading the meditation nodded to me and mouthed, *"Close your eyes."* I just shook my head and mouthed back, *"No."* My Reiki master sensed something was not right and so she swapped places with me. It appeared that the lady sitting next to me was going through a rough time and it was just her negativity, but it was too strong for me, as I had only just been attuned. Another lesson learned; I have not been back since.

I left after that and Elsie said that it was the right thing to do. All the way home, though, I could feel the negativity and it was not nice.

After my attunement I had started to get an awful headache, one like I've never had before or since. I couldn't sleep. I didn't sleep for days; I just snatched the odd hour. Every time I closed my eyes I could see tiny, bright golden lights and then I saw them ... they were tiny angels, I could see them as clear as day. But it wasn't just the tiny angels I was seeing, it was faces, and they looked confused and their eyes were looking around. That scared me too, but Elsie told me not to be scared.

It was then that I started to talk to another angel, who said he was the Archangel Michael, and he would help me. I found myself talking even more to Elsie and Michael. I took sanctuary at the salon and my friend would give me a massage and I would sleep for a brief while. I think that at the time I was too open, but it was not my Reiki master's fault, it had just unleashed something that had been trying to get out for so many years, that it all came at once!

One night I awoke to a most weird sensation – one I would not like to feel again, and know I never will. It was as if something was holding me down. I was told to be quiet and that everything was going to be ok. I was told that Elsie, Ted and my daughter Georgina were there and that something important was happening. It felt as if something was being implanted in me, it was just so intense.

I was absolutely terrified. I remember thinking I was going to die ... I went into the kitchen and started talking to Elsie and

Ted and they were very, very concerned about my wellbeing at the time. They seemed to be flustered themselves. This is the part of the story that will seem very farfetched to you and you will have to make your own judgement on this and me, but I am sure if you spoke to your guides and angels they would assure you that it was very real.

I remember in particular Elsie being very frightened; something big was happening and she said she felt like a small child again, although she was experienced – or so she thought – at this business. I sat down at my kitchen table and it was as if I was sitting next to Elsie. I took her hand and together we sat; it was if we were two people, it was so surreal. Then the mood became very calm and sombre. I knew then that this was going to be big. I found myself having a conversation with my God. She said that for me she was a female energy and so you must excuse me for continually calling her She. God said that Elsie and I would have a very special and unique bond. That Elsie would be not just by my side but also inside, and would be able to see through my eyes when necessary. (I know this sounds like madness but I can assure you I am very sane. I am not possessed, but if necessary, I know that Elsie can manipulate me – all for the greatest, highest good.) God said that I would have to be very strong, that we would both have to be very strong. My journey would be bigger than I could ever imagine, but it would all be perfect. The facial images I had been seeing were lost souls, and God said I had been collecting them for many years and it was time to release them to the universe. She said that I would always do this job, and I would always be protected. The conversation is one that sometimes God will bring up, and it usually starts with, "Who'd have thought that this could all begin in a tiny kitchen sat at a tiny table ..." And yes, I still have conversations with God, but that is not something I talk about as I know that some people do not understand.

The next day, I was on my way to work and I started to talk to my daughter about the whole thing (we worked together). I didn't get to actually go to work that day. We ended up sitting in Sainsbury car park, discussing all sorts of things. Her spirit Guardian Angel is called Nialo and she has a fab relationship with him. He also helps me on occasion, but that is usually when I have a lesson to learn. I am getting wise to him! My daughter is very sensitive like me, and she was getting flustered, and it was then that I just seemed to smack my hand on her head and said, this is for you …. Again, it is the truth, and yet written down, it seems absurd. She then heard God, and God said we all had to talk. It is very apparent that both of us are to be involved in the work that God needs us both to do.

We went to a local beauty spot and there we started to have a five-way conversation involving Elsie, Nialo, Myself, my Daughter and God …. in a car park! It was there that God said that her second daughter was very special to this earth. Please forgive me, because as I am writing this I can see that it all looks like a big fantasy, but it truly isn't. It is harder to write about than I first thought, because I know I could be opening myself up to ridicule and it is not something I am doing lightly.

God said that my granddaughter was a Rainbow child and that she would help other Rainbow children to develop; together, they would help to settle the earth and her energy. My daughter's job is to take care of her and the new little ones. They will come to her while they are still in what I know as the Spiritual Realm (the Universal Light/Energy, or what you will). A few months ago, my daughter was doing a reading for me, when she just stopped. She went very quiet and she spoke softly to me. She said that there were queues of people trying to give me messages but that they had all parted and a very small child had come forward. She sat on my daughter's knee and said, "Are you the mother?" She then showed her a book and they looked at it together. It made my daughter cry. This child is yet to be born.

My job is to continually pass on lost souls, which I do gladly. I've become very used to it; long gone are the days when I am bothered by those beautiful Angels. However, this is not just my journey, it is more of an aside. My job is to protect the Rainbow children; it is to help them to develop, regardless of whether or not we shall actually meet. I believe that I shall work with them and maybe even run a type of school. I have been told that I will know the true Rainbow children. I have absolutely no idea as to how and when, I just know. I have been to see other mediums and they have confirmed this, but I am well aware that God has her plans and sometimes I just have to go with the flow.

I also believe that I am here to give advice from a spiritual perspective, not as a medium but as someone who channels spirit. I'm rubbish at saying, "Dead Auntie Mary wants to say Hi." I'm better at talking to my clients about how they can, if they choose, overcome their hurdles, or just let them know that someone has seen them struggle and maybe I describe what they've been through. I am guided by Elsie, but I have been told there are too many people trying to talk to me all day and that she stops them, because if I were to listen it would drive me mad!

We were both told that the next Rainbow grandchild will be coming in the year that my Granddaughter is five, but we were led to believe that things are moving swiftly and that it will be before then.

My Granddaughter is very special; she is very sensitive, but she is also a normal little child. She is well taken care of. Just recently, I have seen a more spiritual side coming out of her. She is indeed as we call her, a "little witch". Although spirit say she is just a little bit demanding, and we have to keep her in check, they also say she is special!

I don't know where or what's next, I just know it will be. My life has changed dramatically these past two and a half years. When I thought I couldn't carry on I have been uplifted, when I have been desperate for money, it has come. I have faith and I totally believe that I am being taken care of. Things just seem to flow. I have completed my level 2 Reiki and I love working like that. I still say I don't do readings, but I do.

I have seen miracles with my own eyes, which again would just seem to be fantasy to other people.

I hope as you read Sue's story you thought, 'Wow'. This lady has been truly blessed. Her life's journey was unsettled at first, but as her trust, faith and confidence grew, and Sue accepted all spirit had planned for her. She will touch many hearts while on your earth plane, guiding souls home and their destiny.

Sharon's Story

Harold asked me to write my story; well, here it goes:

I was born in 1960 in a home for unmarried mothers run by nuns. At the age of six weeks I was placed with my adoptive parents. They adopted me because my adoptive mother had lost a lot of children and after her first son was born, she was advised not to have any more naturally for her health. I became the middle child when she gave birth to a second natural child. After that, she had a hysterectomy.

My memories of my childhood are that we were comfortably well off, and I know I never went without material things. Growing up was without incident spiritually, but looking back, there was a life event when I was around nine years of age. This event changed my life's path and I believe it was an earth angel who helped me.

I was nine years old struggling with reading, writing and maths, but I loved art and colouring. I was sat at the back of the classroom struggling with my lessons. We had a new head teacher and she picked up that I was dyslexic, and eventually they discovered I had maths blindness too. Even my father, who was a maths teacher, struggled to help me. The head teacher changed my life; I had one-to-one time with her and know I became more confident while under her wing. A lost child, she took me out of the classroom, and she brought on my speech, reading and writing. I will always remember this lady's kindness and how she redirected me on my life's path at this tender age. My maths never really got better but I did eventually achieve an O Level C grade in English so I could get into Art College.

My childhood was secure but I don't remember hugs and cuddles. I realised in my early teens that my parents were heavy drinkers (it emerged later they were both alcoholics). I have memories of fights and unhappy times between them. My mother and father were very controlling, but my mother more so. They seemed to be racist too. I was told not to mix with Indian girls, but I had an Indian friend at school, who my parents never new about. I never learned why they had this attitude, as I did not feel like this. At seventeen, I was told they wanted me to marry a doctor or dentist and never bring home a coloured man. I was encouraged to go into the Young Conservatives, but never enjoyed it. I did not realise my life was not my own until I went to college.

At the age of nineteen I went to art college in my hometown of Loughborough. Wow – this changed my life. Mixing with people from all walks of life, colour and race – I loved the experience. I realised what a controlled, safe upbringing I had had. Things were going quite well at college until I met my future husband Chris. Sadly, he was never good enough for my parents and one day they made me choose between them and him. Well, I chose my boyfriend and yes, we are happily married, it's our thirtieth anniversary this year. I moved in with my Chris in my second year of college and we helped each other through it. I worked hard in a pub, and in my third year Chris got a job as he had graduated by then. He supported me so I did not have to work in my third year, and I successfully completed my course.

The first time I met Chris's parents was at their home. It was Christmas time, there was a huge real tree, a real log fire and Christmas was celebrated on Christmas Day. My parents celebrated it on Christmas Eve, with an artificial small tree. I never liked this, as everyone else I knew did not do this. I remember asking my mother why one year, and she said it was because that is how the queen does it.

My life with Chris was good and I had recognised Chris was my rock and soul mate even back then. I did become estranged from my parents; it was so hard to hold a relationship with them. Chris and I lived many happy years together, being successful in our careers. We had our first child in 1993, and our second in 1996. Having the children did break some barriers with my parents and brought us a bit closer to them.

The next main era of my life that was life-changing was the birth of my first child. I was diagnosed with mild postnatal depression, but I soon realised it was more my isolation that was causing me to feel down. We were in Edinburgh at this point in our lives and our families were in Leicester in the Midlands. When I went back to my job after the birth, I was made redundant, and we then decided to move to be near our families, and my sister in law and her children. I realised later in life that this event was meant to happen; as it was time we needed to be near our families.

In January 1996, I had my second child in Leicester. Not long afterwards, my father and Chris's dad became quite ill. My father pulled through but sadly, Chris's dad passed away in the June of 1996. Not long after this, his brother emigrated to Canada and his sister to Denver, USA. On top of this, Chris's mum developed a form of blood cancer. Then Chris got offered a fantastic job opportunity in Bristol, which we could not afford to turn down. So in the space of fifteen months we had a lot of emotional upset and our family unit really changed.

During this time, I had struggled day to day after having my second son. I would go to the doctor, and he would say it was grief and lots of changes, so I'd plodded on. Then we moved to Bristol. When – wham bam – it all hit me. We rented a house on the edge of a village, knowing no one. My symptoms got worse, and then one day I remember sitting on the stairs, and my two young sons were looking at me, asking mummy if she was ok. I remember thinking, I can't cope anymore, and thought the only way out was to end my life; I was suicidal. I had no thought of harming my children; I was just in such a dark, dark place. But something made me think, this can't go on, and I rang my husband at work, who could not talk to me as he was in a meeting. Something made me look in the old phone book and I rang some helpline; to this day I can't remember which one, but after sobbing down the phone a voice calmly told me to get to my local doctor's surgery that day. I knew this was nearby up my road, so I rang them, sobbing again, and she told me to come straight down. I know now this was my guide, and angels guiding me.

So with two kids in tow, I plodded off to the doctor's, and all I could do when I got in there was cry. I was put in a side room, where I waited for a doctor. Eventually, a very nice lady doctor came in, asked some questions and told me to wait, and she would see me ASAP. She decided to send me to the hospital to see a psychiatrist. I was terrified, and I was imagining being locked up and my kids being taken away from me. At my appointment, after lots of tears, the psychiatrist diagnosed postnatal depression. He said the medication and care would come from my surgery with his recommendation. I was relieved what I had was treatable from my home. I then had a wonderful, kind health visitor who came in every day to check on my children and me; I started on medication and counseling sessions. My husband, bless him, was a bit lost in all this but was supportive, as he had to be at home on the days I had my counseling.

The counseling revealed some suppressed childhood memories of being mentally abused by my mother, which had carried on into adulthood. Also, there was the loss of a secure family group I had in Chris's family, as well as the hormones being all mixed up. It took me three to four years to find my old self, but I did get there.

I did eventually lose my adoptive mother to cancer; she was taken very quickly. My brother rang me with the sad news that she had not long to live. I had not seen her for a while and had never made up over past events. I went to the hospital on my own to visit her. I remember walking up to her bed, the woman I had feared and been hurt by was lying there in a very vulnerable state, dying. All the hurt and pain I held in my heart washed over me, I just sat down and held her hand, no words were needed, we just looked at each other and knew there was forgiveness. I was so upset after leaving the ward, a Macmillan nurse took me to a room and I poured it all out to her. She made me realize I had done what was needed, to come for my mum to die in peace, and for me to move on in my life. I know Macmillan nurses are earth angels. I went back home and my mother passed away about a week later.

Life settled down and in 2009 we decided to take an office space ten minutes from home for our advertising business. This was the start of my light worker's journey. I shall come back to this in a bit; first I'll share my spirit experiences in my life, and beliefs to this point.

My religious experiences were from a young age based on brownies and guides, but for some reason it never sat comfortably with me. When I started to be aware of spirit I also became aware of knowing, for example, that I believed Jesus was from above us, from the skies, but was an alien and came in a spaceship. I knew UFOs were real, and witnessed one in my hometown of Loughborough in the late 1970s. I was also very drawn to the story of Atlantis and any sci-fi films. I also felt that so far in my life, my experience of religions had been based on fear, not love.

I don't remember having spirit experiences when young; mine started in my early teens.

The first one was when I went on holiday with my parents to a cottage. I must have been about thirteen. As soon as we pulled up, I took one look at the cottage and felt fear when looking at the windows. It was as if I was being watched. This got worse as I entered the lounge and the kitchen area. I was supposed to sleep downstairs on my own but was terrified. I felt some terrible event had taken place here, which was connected with a female. I discovered on this trip that my mother believed in spirit, and as my behaviour was so unusual, they let me sleep upstairs with my younger brother. I did not feel the fear upstairs. Years later I discovered a photo of the cottage amongst my parents' photos and it brought back all those fears. I did not keep the photo, as I did not want the reminder of this experience.

The second experience was when my older brother went to look at Southampton University. I was around fourteen years old. While he was being interviewed my mother and I went to look round the high street. The experience was unusual. I remember waiting to cross the road at a crossing. Then the whole picture I was seeing changed. I was looking at older buildings, horse-drawn carriages, the fashion was eighteenth century, and I saw a young slave girl with her owner. I then heard a voice calling my name; it was my mother. I felt quite dazed and frozen to the spot, I never forgot that experience.

My third one happened when I was eighteen. I got a job in a

pub. I worked in the public bar; there was a narrow standing space behind the bar. About two weeks into the job, I was standing behind the bar, waiting for a customer to serve, when I felt two hands placed on my hips and thought someone was trying to squeeze by; I was pushed forward, but there was no one there. Oh my, was I shaken up. Turned out the place was thought to be haunted, and the area I worked was the most active. A figure was often seen walking along that bar area late at night. I left the pub not long after that.

Over these years, I did start to develop feeling in houses of spirit presence, and sensing things in atmospheres, and I realised I was an empathic, sensing people's feelings and emotions.

The fourth main one was in my late twenties. We had moved into our first owned home, a very cute terraced house in Cheltenham. A few months in, we decided to put some stairs into our basement and make it a usable space. Not long after, I started to dream of a man standing in our doorway and looking into our room; sometimes, I was not sure if I was awake or asleep when I saw him. One night, I was woken with the feeling that someone was leaning over the bed, and then on it. We had a piano in our dining room and I always felt someone was behind me, just watching. I had two cats; sometimes they would watch the stairs and then run at high speed out of the cat flap. The funny thing was that once I accepted his presence, I was not scared. I looked into the history of our house. The next door house used be a stable for coaches that dropped guests off at the big houses nearby, and the coachmen used to use the basement of our house while they waited. We did find animal bones in the old fireplace in the basement, which was evidence of cooking. I feel he was part of this era, just popping back in to see us. My husband never saw or felt anything, but a friend who stayed once saw him at the top of my stairs, she told me a while after her visit, and I had not told her about the spirit presence.

My fifth experience took place when we rented a flat in Edinburgh; we were in a Georgian building on the top floor. Sometimes when I would climb up to the flat, I would hear the echo of children laughing. I thought the flat under me must have kids, but there were no children in the block. I did realise that our flat would have been the old children's nurseries or schoolrooms. I always felt ok in the flat, it was just like I was hearing sounds from the past.

The other notion I mentioned earlier was that I believed Jesus was an alien, who was different from mankind, with great healing powers. I never knew where this came from, but it was always there. When my son was at primary school, he one day told me they were talking about Jesus and asked my opinion. I told him my thoughts on Jesus, as I believed in always being honest with my kids. What I did not realise was that they were running a school assembly on the subject. I had a call one day that turned out to be the day of the assembly. The head teacher was quite shocked to hear what had come out of my son's mouth when he had put up his hand and said: "My mum says Jesus is an alien" etc. I was Chair of Governors at the time, but decided to be honest with the head teacher and tell her my beliefs. Nothing else was ever said on the subject!!!

In the years leading up to my light worker path, I believe I was either too busy or ill to be susceptible. The only thing that kept happening was a dream. My dream was that I'd be in a drawing room; there were wooden floors, large French wooden doors leading out into a garden, and a grand piano. I could also be in a hall and landing, with paintings on the walls. There was also a bedroom I would not enter. As part of this dream, I would go to a black gravestone in what I knew was a family plot. I always felt this was not from my lifetime.

Now back to 2009 and our office move. We took up residence in an office unit; next door there was a wonderful lady, who was a holistic healer. She had a table and chairs outside and we started chatting over tea breaks. I told her about my repetitive dream; she just knew I needed a past lifetime regression. She was right; my dream was from a past life. I believe this dream and experience were given to me, so I linked with her to tell her my stories. She was a Reiki master, and she suggested I did my Reiki level one; WOW – that experience changed my life. With the Reiki one I had to heal myself, and I forgave my mother for the years of heartache, which allowed me to move on.

I then did my Reiki two. I sat in her Reiki and meditation circles for a couple of years, and in this time, my interest in mediumship grew. This led to attending a workshop about mediumship, where we connected to spirit. What I did not realise was that I opened up a door to the spirit world and they would not leave me alone. I struggled with it, and with my lack of experience, I did not know how to deal with them. My Reiki master suggested that I shut down, and told me how to do this. I carried on in the Reiki circle. I had not thought of setting up a holistic business, as I seemed to be on more of a spiritual path with my Reiki. I also could not get my head around charging for Reiki, as spirit gives us this healing, channeling through us. I later learned that a lot of new Reiki babies feel this, but the spirit world want to spread this healing and us to earn a living from it.

Not long after this, I had a very accurate, mind-blowing reading with a medium called Marcus. At the end I was told to go on my creative path, and spirit would be waiting for me to start my mediumship path again. Well, I was starting on my dream of making books to sell, and laughed at the mediumship journey. I eventually left my Reiki circle and moved forward on my creative path. I did continue my interest in Reiki and the angels, and was guided to read angel and medium books as well as inspiring stories.

As always, spirit knew my path. A couple of years ago I joined a gym to get fit; in the first few weeks I met a lady from my past, and although we got on well, she seemed sad and down. Every time I saw her I got Reiki, Reiki, Reiki, I knew she needed Reiki. I held myself back for a bit, as I had not practiced Reiki for a while and was not sure of what her reaction would be. Then one day I took the plunge and asked her if she had considered Reiki, and to my surprise she jumped at the chance. This is when my light bulb went back on, as I call it.

I felt I wanted to practice Reiki and retrigger my mediumship. To begin with, I offered Reiki free to my friends and family to build my confidence, which was lacking at this time. I was then drawn to see a local medium called Berni on platform. I was inspired by her and felt very drawn to her energy. I contacted her and asked if she taught mediumship and how to do it safely. She put me in touch with a place called Heaven Sent Spiritual Centre, run by the lovely Maria. One Thursday night I took myself off to her open development group. When I arrived at the location it was situated at riding stables; I had to laugh because I'm allergic to horses. I walked into the centre and was made so welcome; I knew straight away I was in the right place and never looked back – and I was nowhere near a horse. Berni has become one of my mentors; I attend her workshops regularly, always being inspired and always learning. I set up my own business in March 2015, practicing healing, mediumship and meditation. Now, I have also started teaching workshops; it is an amazing experience seeing others develop and grow, as you have yourself.

There is so much more I could write, but this is the basic outline of my life's path so far. I did question why it was so late in my life that I found this wonder of spirit and working with them. But I know as I progress with my Bengalrose business that what I have learnt I can share with others and help them. It has given me great understanding of myself and I know now that all our paths are different. Never compare yourself with others – we are individual but we are all as one. You can heal, forgive and climb over great obstacles in life. Rejoice when others achieve, send healing to those that need it. I have learned to be ME; when you find yourself you can then be the best you can be.

Thank you, Sharon, for writing your story for me. You have many more, I know, that people can learn from, but what you have written shows the things that have happened in your life, that link you simply with spirit on your life's path. This link slowly grew, introducing you to us slowly and as your life calmed down, the link got stronger. Everything you experienced in your life led to that point as you put it, 'your light bulb came back on moment'. Now you can take what you have learned and pass it on to fellow mankind so they can learn from you. Thank you, my friend; we look forward to our continued journey with you and continuing your education with us.

Chapter 6

The best of mankind

You are awesome

As I conclude our messages for you all I would like to tell you how strong and magical mankind is, and how if you believed in yourselves, your world would shine out into the universe like a pure sparkling jewel. You are all so unique and have an inner and outer beauty unique to each and every one of you.

I know that spiritualist light workers among you have accepted our spirit being race as part of you; you see we have merged together in to unique beings and understand the reasons for this. As the rest of world sees this bond, the benefits and accepts us, we know the earth vibration will rise towards creating the fifth dimension beings you can be. There is nothing to fear my friends our relationship can only grow, get stronger and more awesome.

Our wish is to bring positivity, healing, love and support to humanity. We wish to shine our love vibration down on you all, offering guidance to help mankind understand our world and what you could achieve if you opened up to us. Humans are developing into the most amazing beings, with mix of spirit and other off-world influences. No harm has ever been wished on you from any of us in Utopia, we are not capable of it. Your well fare and true being is at the forefront of every action we take, we want you to learn from us as we learn from you.

Each and every one of you will complete the circle of life, returning home to us, while living on earth as an individual, in a unique existence, which will be perceived in different ways by your fellow mankind.

I feel you all need inspiring, my friends, so I requested a couple of questions to be asked through your modern day social media; some of you kindly replied, and the replies are below. The first question was: *"Ok, I have a question for you all: what do you see as a strength in mankind?"*

Your answers: forgiveness, acceptance, honesty, freethinking, love, kindness, compassion, patience, tolerance, tenacity, courage, generosity, integrity, creativity, empathy, harmony, loyalty and friendship.

Wow! These are powerful words and is it not wonderful to see, as you all have, these strengths within you; even better – I am sure that as you read this list, you are adding more positive words in your heads.

You also used positive quotes in some of your answers, my friends, which are inspiring. I thought this quote was very wonderful: *"To make a conscious choice at every moment in how we want to feel and be. The choice is always ours."* As we have already said, you have free will and thinking, the choice is always yours; some of you just need to learn to live using the strengths of mankind, in love and light with our guidance, and you will find your inner strength and power.

There were other quotes I loved; I have put my thoughts down below for you all.

I would like to comment on the quote: *"Imagination & the ability to see beauty wherever that might be."* Mankind has the most amazing imagination; combined with your intelligence, this has enabled mankind to achieve great art, designs, architecture, writings and much more.

This leads me to the words 'over-imaginative', which are used for children or adults who are more open to seeing unusual things, such as, for example, invisible friends. Many a human has paid a price for this gift; they have had to hide their ability or been locked away as a mad person over the centuries. The things they see are spirits from our realm, aliens or elemental beings. When they interact like this, they receive messages and inspiration. Throughout your history, some of you, as we touched on in an earlier chapter, manage to tap into the universe's knowledge and invent and create well beyond their time. Remember Leonardo De Vinci!

Children often mention invisible friends; as well as them seeing spirit from our realm, there are those amongst you blessed with the ability to see the elemental beings as well. They live in a dimensional plane on earth, amongst your rich beauty of plant life. There are four basic elements of nature: fire, air, earth and water. Within each of the four elements there are **nature spirits** that are the spiritual essence of that element.

They are made up of etheric substance that is unique and specific to their particular element. (What is Etheric energy? It refers to a type of very fine matter or substance. It is all around us, and it permeates all physical matter and space throughout the universe.)

Elemental beings are living entities, which often resemble humans in shape, but inhabit a world of their own. The terms fairies, pixies and goblins are a few of the names you have given them. They help to look after Mother Earth and have learned to adapt to mankind's pollution, as this does affect any being that interacts with your earth. They have shifted their habitats to safe areas of their beloved Mother Earth, and they do interlink with your world as spirit can. They also wish, as some of mankind does, to treat nature and earth creatures better, letting the wild animals be free to live as they were born in their natural habit. They also want you to manage your trees and all nature better, and they silently work alongside us, helping your earth. They bring joy and mischievousness to those that can see them, and their hearts are true and full of love.

Another powerful quote I loved from you was: *"Triumph over adversity."* Some of you have chosen lessons to learn in your life on earth that need you to be very strong, so you have the strength to triumph over some of the hardest emotional and physical obstacles. Mankind has always had this power; you now need to take this inner strength and learn to live as one.

Look at others as you would wish them to look upon you,
their eyes will always tell the truth; always be true
to yourself and others; see them through their eyes,
deep into their souls, then trust your intuition.

Following on from the main question I then asked a second question *"Ok my friends what do you not like about your fellow mankind?*

Your answers: dishonesty, ignorance, intolerance, hate, cruelty, greed, callousness, evil and blindness.

What I loved to see about this was that fewer people responded, and the positive answers outweighed the negative. These questions were asked by a light worker, amongst a group of like-minded people and their friends and families, so perhaps you would expect this. If we asked the same questions in different parts of the world, I know the balance would be different. This makes our hearts sing though, when we see such positive feedback from humans.

There was another quote I would like to respond to as well from this second question:

"Cruelty to animals and no regard for nature or its animals." We feel, as you work towards all living as one in pure heart, that mankind will also look at the way you treat your animals for food. The pressure of money gains and feeding mass populations has taken over your caring nature for these animals.

For thousands of years, mankind has killed animals to eat, and we have loved the societies that have appreciated the animals' worth and life, who thank them for giving theirs. We are not saying don't eat meat; but less meat is better for your human body makeup; mankind needs more food grown organically. When you cleanse your body you cleanse your soul, and you become healthier and happier, which lifts your vibration.

You all need to work together to free all imprisoned wild life to nature reserves, where they can be protected. Mankind has started to work towards this, but sadly, more of your wild life will become extinct before this is fully achieved; but action now will save some species. The legacy of 'extinct animals', will be just images for your history books and will be what you pass on to your children and grandchildren. What will your answer be when they ask you: *"Why are they extinct?"* This saddens my heart.

Part of the big picture of looking after your animal kingdom is how you grow your food. Your food chain can be helped with the simple things. For example, those of you with land and gardens could grow vegetables; you can also build every new home to harness the energy of the sun and wind. Over time, this will help Mother Earth heal. Organic foods are what mankind needs, so steer away from pesticides and try to control your crops from seeds. We understand that as the human race has exploded across your planet, mankind has felt the need to intervene in nature to sustain yourselves, but you can do this organically, with the world acting as one. This is a big task and will take time, but start in your own back yards, my friends, and the word will spread.

We would also like to add that from amongst your plant life, nature does offer on your earth natural medicine cures. Try to explore these more, and you will be able to shed your man-made drugs. Ask us for guidance and help – we can lead you to trained holistic healers that work alongside your modern medical practitioners. Sadly, my friends, man-made medicines mean huge money for some humans, so there are elements of your society that do not like the holistic way; but you will prevail.

I felt these two quotes were worth exploring too: *"Those who judge before exploring the whole story"*, and: *"They have eyes but cannot see."* Your eye vision is a blessing and can be used to help access your pathway in life, but you also have an inner ability to look at things deeper with the third eye, and not take them at face value. Don't listen to others and use their judgement as your own. Take a deep look at the person or situation in question. You will be surprised at what you will find – they are quite often not as they seem.

What really made me smile is when I saw this answer: *"There's nothing to dislike ... We are soul mates x."* Would it not be amazing if mankind could only have answers like to this when asked: *"Ok my friends – what do you not like about your fellow mankind?"* One day, my friends.

Our wish for you - To bring your world back into the light with Spiritualism

I have written spiritualism into the message of the book already. My aim is to guide you to your knowledge in your world, and for you to educate yourselves; also to understand our realm and what we wish to achieve from working with you on planet Earth. My hope is that the words in this book will lead you to understanding yourselves better, and what is behind spiritualism in our world. We wish you to embrace us in to your lives and other alien beings too.

So what is spiritualism my friends? Your words simply phrase it as: *"A system of belief or religious practice based on communication with the spirits of the dead, especially through mediums."*

But it is much more, my friends. One of your modern day western spiritualism groups has created these basic seven principles under western world spiritualism. They are based on your understanding of the spirit world from your light workers' experiences and communications with us. We call this the ethos of spiritualism, the energy atmosphere you live in, and how you live vibrates out all around you in earth energy. Living by the spiritualism guide below will pull in love and light, and lift the vibration around you.

- The Fatherhood of God
- The Brotherhood of Mankind
- The Communion of Spirits and the Ministry of Angels
- The Continuous Existence of the Human Soul
- Personal Responsibility
- Compensation and Retribution Hereafter for all the Good and Evil Deeds done on Earth
- Eternal Progress Open to every Human

There is one we would like to be added so you can bring our wisdom and teachings to your children. Encourage your children to look beyond 'the now moment' and think out of the box, lifting their mind to fulfill their potential for the greater good of all mankind.

- The responsibility of the spiritual education of mankind

Philosophy is a key part of spiritualism teachings, my friend. A lot of you will think you have to be a brain box to understand or be part of anything to do with this word 'Philosophy'. When your mediums connect to us, we can pour our philosophy out into you in ways you can understand. But you can all have the power to connect to the great knowledge pot of wisdom and philosophy, and when you do – my, how your lives will change. With each individual we always make sure you receive this knowledge in a way each of you can understand, as you are all different, and we are happy to do this for you.

As with all forms of belief systems, spiritualism has been categorized by mankind, and placed under religion. Mankind does this with everything in their lives; as you live within the third dimension order of things, you need to set everything in its place through fear, and the power of controlling your feelings. At the moment, we feel there is an advantage of this; we can see that mankind needs this category to help you build the confidence to drive on the spiritual side of life and spread the word to others; there are those that will need this category system for a comfort zone until they discover their ascension path, and ride above the third dimension way of life vibration and living.

We are working with and inspiring some of you to bring positivity and uplifting ways to improve your work and home lives. For example, as well as working with light workers, we are also working with life coaches, business coaches and teachers. Our aim is to bring our positive, uplifting message to mankind in anyway it will be accepted. If mankind can be inspired to make positive changes in their way of thinking, in any area of their lives, this will then spread into other areas of their lives. They will attract in more positives, and it will become a way of being. Please see the BIG picture my friends, it is like a painting by numbers. Fill in the gaps and you will build a beautiful, whole, enlightened picture for mankind's future. Yes spiritualism is behind this way of thinking, we want this to be away of life, not a worship pattern like existing religions.

All religions connect with the great source of love and light, under the different names of the God they worship. As I have already said, some of the religions have lost that original spark of the divine that triggered them, and it is now long forgotten. These religions are on a path of fear, worry and neglect of their divine paths on love and light.
Spiritualism can be the base for all religions; it will help guide all of them back to that spark that triggered their original beliefs long ago. So go forth, my friends – spread the word, and bring

mankind back to the first spark of the divine love and spirit.

Time is of the essence in your world; to stop the meltdown mankind is causing on Mother Earth. From Utopia, we have seen a shift in mankind over the last few years, with more of you seeing the love and light. We also see that a lot of you are still afraid to reveal your new feelings and beliefs in case of ridicule. **YOU** must take this leap of **TRUST,** step out of your shell, and tell the world what you know and believe in. Yes, my friends, when you reveal your belief, there will be those that will move out of your life. But to counterbalance this, you will attract like-minded people to you. Eventually, these spiritualist groups will merge and blend with other religions, with all of you becoming one. There will be frictions while achieving this path, but your trust, strength and convictions will see you through.

If you take this leap of faith and take it one step at a time, you will be amazed at the difference you can make. A lot of you know what to do, but take no action to help mankind or your animal kingdom to survive in equality and as one.

I am sorry if you feel this is one big lecture, but what I want you to realise is that if you ask your guides and angels to help, we will leap into action to support and guide you.

Chapter 7

Inspirational quotes to lift your mind and inner being

Your voice

Your path will find the right words for your voice.
You will find the right voice for your path.

The vibration is from the soul;
the tone is from your heart.

Pitch this right and we hear,
answering you in a chorus of song.

Hear our voices, loved ones, as we hear yours.
All will be clear and true to you.

Utopia is heaven, heaven is Utopia, beauty, paradise and pure love, but these are just words, your soul holds the known beauty of heaven my friends. Your home will always be our realm, but when you return to us, you will always carry a small part of your life's you choose to live on planets and other realms. The essence of that life form, their language will always be a part of you. Every life you choose to live is part of your learning path and will always hold new inspirations for your soul, bringing them back home. The path you will always aim to tread while in that life is for, positivity, inspiration and wisdom so you can trigger the light bulb moment of finding love and light and spirit to guide you.

As part of your journey we would like you to then be our voice and pass on what you have learnt to fellow mankind. This can be as simple as being kind and understanding to your fellow mankind and nature, or to stand up and go out into the world with your voice and teach. I have been inspired while writing this book to write quotes to guide you, inspiring your souls and bringing you into the love and light of our world. Why? Because we want you to be our ambassadors' for your world, we want you to be our voice reaching out to your fellow mankind and raise awareness of spirituality and the positive way of thinking. The easy way would be for me to fill these pages full of images from your beautiful planet and solar system, but I set myself the challenge to achieve this with words to inspire your minds and imaginations.

Part of the spiritual journey mankind takes while on earth is to be inspired by what surrounds them in their lives. Key to being successful on your life plan is to have a soul and mind that is fueled with wisdom, philosophy and inspired words. You would recognise this as a basis for Spiritualism on earth.

As you know, we communicate telepathically in Utopia; I suppose you could say our thoughts are a language we use, that you would understand as words. Just to remind you, we exist in love and light in a fifth dimensional state, surrounded by positive energy instead of the negative energy that surrounds a lot of you living in your third dimensional state, so our use of our language is always positive, uplifting and all for the greater good. Your negative words collect in your ethos, or energy fields, this makes the layers harder for us to penetrate, as we are a positive, uplifting energy form. It's a bit like a soft white feather trying to get through some sand, trying to drop through to the bottom so it can be seen; we have to work hard to penetrate this matter. If mankind could just lift their vibration a bit more, amazing things would start to happen.

We will not give up, as we want to inspire your soul and mind with inspirational words, thoughts and love.

Our spirit realm inspires writings all around your world daily, and has done for centuries. As a species, you are unique in the way you use words to bring down others or inspire them to better things. I don't like to mention negativity in a book that is to inspire mankind, but if you all took a look at the way you use your languages, taking away the negative words and replacing them with positive, you would see a great change in mankind. It is not just the words you use but also the way you say them, my friends.

Also remember that in your lives, words are not always needed. A look, a touch, a hug, an embrace – these are unsaid words, and your intention can be reflected in your eyes and all can be forgiven without words. A held hand, an arm around a shoulder, and just being in a grieving person's space will, with the right intentions, let them know you love them. Tears, smiles and emotions can wash away any doubt they have that you care. So imagine, my friends, with these thoughts that trigger these positive vibrations, and spoken, powerful, positive words, the messages you could send out to mankind to raise their vibrations.

Using positive words and phrases will change your lives for the better and this inspired me to write quotes of inspiration. The universe is full of positive energy and your angels and guides want you to be part of this positive energy and love. You will change your lives with this new way of talking and thinking. You will notice how people will be drawn to you more and your day-to-day life will be lifted and more sparkly and sunny.

When you have a negative thought, throw it out of the ballpark, then say to yourself "Love and Light". If you find yourself having a not so nice thought about a situation or someone, stop and send them a loving healing thought. You will become happier, feel better in your inner being and will have a more positive outlook on all you do.

As you develop this new mind-set of positive thinking, others will take notice and start using it too. As we have already said, teach it to the children in your lives – they are our future and our hope for a more positive and peaceful world. They are mankind's future.

YOU are YOU. This change of thought and lifestyle takes a while to achieve, as you have to unravel some old habits. But your angels and guides walk beside you, so ask them for help, support and healing on your journey with this positive outlook challenge you set yourselves.

I have decided to separate the quotes and inspirational words into areas to help you all to know when to call up on them, as they are needed.

Rising out of pain and grief

When mankind faces the loss of a loved one in death, human or animal, you naturally go through a grieving process. When a loved one leaves you to pass home you miss their essence and physical presence here on earth. A piece of your heart goes with them. You will grieve for their loss and ask questions like why? What if? Some of this grief can be regrets, unsaid words, and sorries that were not said. The regret of that pain can eat you up. The grief of losing someone close rips at the human heart.

You have to fight the battle of hiding yourself away in your grief, asking why them and being angry at the world, or come out fighting and face the world around you. Remember my friends while in your own grief there is others around you dealing with the loss as well. Part of the healing for the human spirit is to embrace your loved ones and friends, draw them near and let them give their time and help to you, as you will all have needs and ways to deal with grief. Stay open to the world around you and you will heal with time. When spirit returns home, I know they do not want you to grieve or carry pain in your hearts.

Also you might need healing from suffering abuse and neglect in your life's and carry pain from these life events with you, these need to be released so you can heal.

Your spirit team and healers will be round you with just a thought, trying to heal you and help you move forward with your lives. The time you all need for this will vary and various things will help, such as hugs, being surrounded by loved ones, kind words and support. If you have some one that's has lost someone in your life now or in the future take the time to send them some kind words or a quote for inspiration. This lets them know you care and are thinking of them and inspired words from spirit will help them move forward on their life's path. You will know with your intuition what words they need at that point in time, they will stand out to you from these pages.

Time is the healer

To be whole is to be honest with your self.
Time distorts memories and trust.
The memory left is not what truly was.

To trust is based on true self-worth.
Move on forward, do not look back.
Your memories are left back in time.

Your past will always be there with you
Bring forward the love, not the hurt
Time is your healer; just trust in us.

Time holds old stories,
move forward to write your future story,
and don't relive the pages.

Joy

To find joy in your heart,
go out into Mother Nature,
find time to sit and enjoy her tune,
it will sing in your heart.

Make a change

Today is the day I make a change.
I am moving on to new warmth and light,
I do not want to be where my heart is breaking.

Today is the day I make a change.
I know my true friends will move forward with me,
walking alongside me on my path.

Today is the day I make a change.
I will try new things; have new experiences,
I am growing in strength and love.

Today is for ME I have made the change.
My heart is lifted from the sadness if left behind,
I smile again with new Trust all will be well.

Today is for YOU make the change.
Move forward; don't hold back in the past,
The future is yours, walk forward shining.

Stay in the sunshine

As you rise up out of the darkness into the sunshine my friend,
you are blossoming like a pure white lily flower.

Your smile is lighting up many faces and affecting many hearts,
don't let your smile ever fade.

As you stride forward with new-found confidence in life
and love in your heart, you will find your path.

Your inner beauty is your soul and essence of the divine;
a spark of goodness is what you will find inside your soul.

You know the answers, my friend; we are all here with you,
guiding, supporting, loving and smiling as you progress.

So stay in the sunshine, smile out to the world, radiating your
inner happiness and you will change all of those that see your
spark of love and light.

Blessings my friend, walk your path with trust and love.

Gather your loved ones near

Hold out your arms and gather your loved ones near.
They will give you strength my friends.
They are your inspiration,
your listeners and your support network.
Their love is your love.
Your light is their light.
Blend and be as one, you will know peace.

Healing

Healing is forgiveness
Healing is accepting your past
Healing is letting go of the pain
Healing is letting others help you
Healing is listening to yourself
Healing is moving on past
Healing is a teardrop
Healing is a simple smile
Healing is a hug
Healing is a moment of time

Inner healing

Inner healing comes from within the soul.

Your heart is love; your mind can be the disease.

If you let your mind run in a negative thought pattern,
your body will be dragged down with it.

When negative thoughts come in, hit them out the ballpark
with a big bat in your head, and think of someone
you love or a favourite moment in time.

Your body will start to fill up with positive energy,
lifting your inner being. This then sends positive waves round
your
body, healing it as they go.

The Circle of life

Think, my friends, of your life's path from the first breath you
take, until you take your last. It's not a never-ending circle;
there is a beginning and end while on earth.

Fill this circle of life with love, compassion,
empathy, kindness and strength. Be one of life's inspirers,
leaders, and the best example mankind can offer.

You have to fill your own circle up, don't think others
will do it for you, my friends; this is your story and your path;
live it.

As you fill your circle up, draw others into it with love
and kindness.

It does not matter how big your circle gets,
as long as it is pure of heart and filled with true values.

So, my friends, live your life to the full, let your
circle expand to touch other hearts and inspire them from
your soul.

Be happy, positive and true

Do not hurt those near to your heart,
look at your actions and theirs.
Do not judge too quickly;
look at them as a whole

If you cannot be together,
pull apart, but keep them in your heart.
Rise above the hurt and forgive,
life is for living and being happy

True love is smiles and happiness,
being together even from a distance.
Help, guide and support each other,
do no tear each other down.

Only you can evaluate you life.
Do you smile, and laugh together?
Trust and have faith in each other,
hold this in your heart and love life.

Look in the deepest part of your soul,
their lie the answers and the way forward.
Be happy, positive and true,
life will bring what is right for you.

Tide of time

Time slips over you like a wave;
let it wash away your fears.
Let it gently soothe your soul
and wipe away your tears.

Feel the gentle ripples on your skin,
feel our touch on your face.
All will resolve in time dear friend
just take life at a timely pace.

As you drift on the tide of time,
you will feel our love and kiss.
We will take away your pain;
your heart will burst with bliss.

So my friends have faith in us,
give over your heart to our light.
You will now shine in the world;
your love has won the fight.

Fragment of time

Life is a fragment of time, healing is a moment in time.

Fragments are part of a jigsaw that can be put together again.

If the jigsaw has a piece missing, it's not far away from you.

Search the space in your heart and you will find it.

Then gently let go of pain and negativity to us.

Now place the missing piece in the jigsaw.

You are now whole and the picture on the jigsaw
is complete and clear.

What do you see?

I AM HERE.
WHERE HAVE YOU GONE?
I am here.
I CAN'T HEAR YOU.
I hear you.
I WANT TO HEAR YOUR VOICE AND TO HOLD YOU
IN MY ARM'S.
I hear your voice.
I hold you in my arms.
I WANT TO WALK BESIDE YOU AND HOLD YOUR
HAND.
I walk each day with you and I hold your Hand.
I WISH YOU WERE HERE.
I am.

(Thank you Susie friend of Sharon for your contribution)

The spirit from with-in

Your human spirit joins with your divine spirit,
both working together to create a unique being.

You link at the moment of conceptions innocence,
a spark of the divine pure in love and light.

You both work tirelessly together to full fill your life's path;
you all have a mission and a message to be sent out to others.

The separation of your spirits is planned when you return home;
the physical presence is then missed by your loved ones left
behind.

They also miss your heavenly spirit, as this was your soul,
the essence of you, and your true self that shone out to others.

There is great joy when you all reunite in the divine home source,
the source of love and light, true knowing and knowledge.

You will wrap your love around each other again my friends
when you all meet to carry on your spirit paths together.

Good byes

The wave of a hand
The smile on your face
The warmth of your heart
The wisdom and grace

Your laughter in the air
Your scent in the wind
Your friendship to me
Your kindness with no end

Today you left me behind
Today my sun does not shine
Today my heart has a crack
Today I know you are fine

You shine from above
You send us your love
You are beyond earth
You fly free like a dove

I know we will meet one day
I will feel your warmth in time
I will see your golden smile
I know I will be with you again

To inspire you on your spiritual path

The more you read that is positive, the more your vibration will
lift; you will learn to speak these words, then you will reflect this
positivity out to others.

You all have a book of knowledge back in our realm. Your life's
journey sits with your spiritual book of knowledge; you travel
through its pages stopping, looking, pausing, absorbing

information and lessons. You flick through the pages of your book, turning down corners as reminders of your place on your path, or to revisit its content later. Your life's book wears, shows creases and slight tears, as the book is well loved. Every page tells a story, every chapter has an ending. Don't skip the pages, as you need to live, absorb and learn from them. So keep reading, my friends, your text is written and your story needs to be told to others.

If you are working to inspire yourself or others then I feel these quotes will help you; they come from us with much love.

Connect

Your higher self is waiting in pure love existence, don't let your earth self let you down.

Smile as you have never smiled before in the mirror, then look at your reflection beaming back at you.

This is how others will see you; when you smile, a beam of light shines in their world.

Don't be afraid to explore new possibilities in your lives, they are what will make you grow.

Faith comes from within yourself. Have faith in your own abilities and the rest will follow.

Your vision
is our vision,
live it,
breath it,
we will be in it.

Abundance of love

Abundance comes from within; it is your kindness,
love and true self

Abundance is your family, friends and animals in your life

Abundance is being safe, warm and nourished

Abundance is security, health and shelter

Abundance is you as a whole and all goodness around you

When you have abundance give it out to those that don't

Live in love and light and you will have abundance

Let go

Do not worry of what might be.
Be in the now and understand yourself.
You, today, are what matters.
Know your true self and values.
The rest will be there for the taking.
Your tomorrow will be your now.
Your now will be in the past.
Let go and be at peace with yourself.

Find your destiny

Whispers of time float around your minds, like the soft gentle wispy clouds floating on a summer breeze. They just float happily, drifting, waiting for the day they are called up on.

When you learn my friends to settle your minds, you will be able to hold out your hands in front you and gently grasp these whispers from the past.

The softness of them will surround you holding you safe and gently nudging you in the right direction.

These whispers of time are your future; the wisdom they hold is what you have lost. Find this wisdom my friends so you can fulfil you destinies.

Angel hugs

As you wrap your arms around the one you love,
the Angels wrap their love around you.

We are the safe, warm feeling of love and security,
the safety net of life for when you tumble.

We are here to guide and help you on your path;
ask and we will be there with you.

Have no doubt or fear as we are near,
call out and we will answer your wishes.

Look for the answers around you in everyday life,
feel our love and strength as we walk beside you.

As we wrap our wings of love around you,
know you are always safe and loved by the angels.

Blossom

Your journeys intertwine, like a vine in a forest.
Forever searching for the light above the darkness.

You will grow fresh shoots on you life's path.
Branching out in to new exciting adventures.

Keep growing towards the sunlight my friends.
Except the changes your growth will bring you.

Trust in the intuition you feel and breath.
Believe your own self worth and beauty.

You are now the great vine in the forest.
You have reached for the stars and shine.

Be strong and true, just be YOU.

To build self-esteem and positivity within you

Part of your journey is to build self-esteem, positivity, and find contentment with yourselves. Contentment comes from within your heart and soul. What is contentment for mankind? It can be watching a sunset, a child at play, a pebble skimming across the water, helping an old lady cross the road, holding your new-born child for the first time, or a simple cup of tea. The question is, my friends, what makes you content? Have you found this yet on your life's path? We know contentment comes from happiness, well-being, living a true, honest life, helping others, guiding others and teaching others.

To aspire and be what you want to be my friend, the confidence lies with in. Your inner spirit is fighting its way through your human mind layers to reach your goals. We connect mind to mind with you, relax, listen, feel and observe us we are all around you. We wait for that break though my friend, define your goals, we will set them in place with your help.

You are all on the path of finding contentment; some of you are nearer to completing this fulfilling experience than others, but you will all get there. When you have the balance within and in the world around your own being, then yes full contentment will be yours. The nearer you get to this goal the more your light will shine; there will be nothing to stop you achieving your dreams. Contentment is the basis of all happiness my friends. Happiness gives you the spark you need to light your own candle and run down your life's path with your bright lights shining.

So have faith my friends in your own abilities and your soul connection, trust we are guiding you into love and light and a positive new world.

You have probably all realised by now that words affect the world around you. But what can also affect you is your memories, words in your head. Memories serve you well, they keep you connected to who you are and your journey on earth so far. Make sure you do not lose sight of YOU – who you truly are, from the pure spirit source. With all your happy memories and positive emotions you hold, this allows you to move forward. All the other memories that hold fear and negativity need to be boxed and the emotion taken away; they will still be there as they are part of you and your path so far, but will not affect you anymore. This is similar to what you experience when you return home to us; the memories are there but any negativity is lifted away, the memories go into our knowledge pot for all to learn from. You can achieve this while on earth, but you have to work with yourself and us to do so.

When you have achieved boxing the old memories and letting go of any emotion, then you will smile again and stride forward into the next happy memory. You are here to learn and develop, aiming to achieve the best for your higher self. This text will soon be a memory – carry it forward with you in time. Faith comes from within your self. Have faith in your own abilities and the rest will follow.

You are awesome

You are you
You let your light shine
You will be strong
You will be wise
You will learn from hurt
You will heal from harm
You know who you are
You need to be you
You are awesome

Light up the world

Light up the world with your smile

This will reflect in others like a mirror

Smiling and laughter is contagious,
be the person that spreads it; all will smile with you

Smile and laugh your way through life x

Turn Dark into light

If you are feeling your days are dark
Pause...
Light a candle and make a wish
Listen...
We are all around you to give you strength
Feel...
Ask for a sign from us to be near
See...
It might be an angel feather
Touch...
We will touch your heart and inspire you
You...
You are loved and precious to us
Light...
Light your candle and shine into your world
Love...
Loves all around you, love yourself.

Shine

Your world showers sadness down on you
that mankind has made and reflects out to you.
Your soul will cry with others' pain and sorrow;
you will shed and wipe away a silent tear too.

Release this pain from your hearts so you can see
the light on your path to travel your journeys.
Yes listen, feel, then send healing wishes to the
suffering and souls that have gone home.

Surround yourself with our love's protection and
live your lives shining your love out to mankind.
A heavenly shield surrounds you to protect you,
we wish you to shine, my friends, and be you.

Be your best

Discover your inner self, your whole being,
your self-worth and true-life values.

Celebrate your strengths and success,
cast out any self-doubts and negativity.

Do not let others pull you down;
you know your truth and who you are.

Strive to gain all knowledge you can,
about life, love and Mother Nature.

Your inner self wants to grow and learn
starting with being you and trusting yourself.

SHINE, my friend x

Moving forwards

The journey of life moves along on the breath of the wind.
Leaves will tumble down before you on your path.

The question is, my friends, do you kick them away?
OR do you stand, observe, admire and hold this gift from nature?

To stand and observe what's around you can become quiet space.
You will recharge and set your mind's thoughts on the right path.

Please watch where you tread in life, like footprints in the sand.
Once you have passed, the sea will wash them away, the moment
is gone.

Don't look back, my friends, always forward on your paths.
Watch for the beauty of what we set before you, signs from
nature. The choice is always yours – where you tread and the path
you take.

Take that moment in time to hold that autumn leaf and be still.

Guidance for your soul

From the moment you are born we guide and protect your soul
from within Utopia. Your life's journey is like a strong tide,
dipping and moving with your world's energy.

Your journey is like pebbles on a beach, the tide swishing back
and forth until you are a smooth pebble. Ripples of water
soothe your surface, taking away unwanted sharp edges. Your
path sometimes feels as if you skim across the water's surface,
not knowing where you will land. But as the pebble drops

through the water, rocking with the tide, our hands are there to catch you. So don't be afraid, my friends, to dip your toes in the water; you will always see where you tread, just trust we are with you. Carry a pebble with you, feel its smoothness and beauty to remind you of TRUST. Just send out the thought and we will be there to smooth your worries away.

Your soul has great depth and absorbs like a sponge, so you will find that words of deep meaning and philosophy will resonate deep inside your body and essence. You will have had experiences when words spoken have greatly moved you; take note of these times and ask yourself why you feel the way you do?

The soul has eyes

Look at others as you would wish them to look upon you, their eyes will always tell the truth.

Always be true to yourself and others; see them through their eyes, deep into their souls, then trust your intuition.

Time is the essence of your existence, look beyond time to find your true self.

Be your true self

Confirmation of who you are is deep within you.

Find yourself to find the confirmation you seek.

To be you, be happy and follow your passions in life.

Move away from harm and those that do not love you.

You will then find yourself and all the confirmation you need.

Eternity of love is yours

Eternity of love is what we all seek.
Open your eyes — love is all around you.

Mother Earth is love, feel it in the air.
Walk your earth and breath it in.

Love is in your children's innocent eyes.
Love is in your human heart.

Your heart can break due to your love.
But love is a treasure to remember.

Love all that is around you in your life.
Look for the positive things in your world.

Love is for Eternity you have it forever.
Just open your eyes to behold love.

True self

Your true self lies within you,
what's on the surface can be a false exterior.

Remember that when you judge people
not all is revealed and as it seems.

To know their true self, dig below the surface,
there will be resistance from past fear & hurt.

Don't judge your fellow man and woman,
always look within and find their true light.

Every human has this torch of love and light,
it just gets lost through fear of the unknown.

Don't judge help them shine their light,
you will find their true value in time.

Today is a new day, my friends.

Push forward with your lives and step away from
the dark into the light.

Every day is a fresh start for you all
to wipe the slate clean.

Cleanse your soul of any negativity and
bring in only positive light.

Treasure those close to your hearts and
let their love in.

Surround yourself with only love, then this
lets you love in return.

Life is a gift, my friends, unwrap it
and live it to the full.

Nurture your soul

Nurturing your souls is key to you travelling towards
a life of light and love.

Kindness, compassion, and empathy are just a few
things that nurture the soul.

Giving out love and receiving love back into your lives
is also a key factor.

Live in the positive energy Mother Earth gives you, lifting your
vibrations towards us.

All these will ignite your soul, and your mind's thinking.
Don't be afraid to speak out your thoughts, passions and
creative ideas.

Think out of the box, my friends, and share these thoughts with
the world. Do not let fellow man hold you back.

Now ignite your soul and shine into the dark parts of your
world, bringing light and love.

Your Ego

Your ego is like orange peel wrapped round you.

If you let the orange stay whole, you never
get to taste the juicy fruit of life.

Learn, my friends, to peel back the ego
and take a bite of the offerings of creation.

Once you master this, the universe and all it
has to offer is yours.

So take the fruits of life, my friends, and leave
the peel behind.

Be our voice

I do often hear mankind say, *"My soul is tired"*. Tiredness comes
in all shapes and forms for you, physical and mental being the
main two throughout your life's journeys. Every day you will
hear people saying, *"I'm tired"*. This could be from long work
hours, family and friends imposing on you, or health, diet and
aloneness – all of these things are a tired way of being.

We know that one small, positive change could lift this
tiredness and start you on a better path. These changes need to
come from within, but it can take courage to take that first step.
Your soul is not tired my friends, it is your own human mind-
set that makes you think this is so.

To be our voice in any form, you will be a light worker to us.
As a light worker, you will often help and guide fellow humans,
to lift this tiredness they feel with in themselves, moving them
on to the next stage of their life's journey. You will need to be

at your best to do our work. So when you feel tired and your energy is low, remember that it is your physical body and mind that needs rest, and do something for YOU, that you enjoy. Lighten your hearts, laugh, sing and be happy, then you will bounce back to our light and continue on your own journey with us.

The only thing that will stop your progression is your ego. The balance is within you all, secure and steady. If you let your ego control your mind it tips the scales causing you to unbalance. Find your inner spirit and take control, the ego will then only be your shadow in time following as reminder of your old self. As your true self emerges, your inner spirit will lead the way, shining your light and voice into the world.

Your soul is always energised and ready to go, so when your body is at 100% you will then be at your best to help and guide other humans to be happy in their outlook on life, and bounce down their life's path, happily spreading their light and love.

Scatter our love

Harness the love around you and take it into your heart.

Nourish this love so it grows and envelops you.

Then scatter your love like seeds out to your fellow man.

As they catch the seeds they will blossom and grow.

They will then share their love with the world.

The love seeds are carried on the winds to unseen people.

As the light and love grows in the shadow of man.

The world will become one in the love and light.

One step at a time

You cannot save the world single-handed, but you can
contribute.

Have positive thoughts every day.
Think: How can I serve for the greater good?

Donate some time to a good cause.
Help Mother Earth and her environment.

Teach someone goodness today.
Listen to those around you.

Accept each other's faults and forgive.
These are all simple thoughts and gestures.

Let them become part of your everyday lives and you
will shine a light into the dark corners of your world.

If we all did this every day, imagine what
a wonderful world it would become;
we just need to unite and be as one.

You are all as one

Live as one
You live in divide
Come together as one
Be whole and true
Love and see as one
Be as one and shine

Live hand in hand
Walk side by side
Learn from each other
Teach each other
Support each other
Guide each other

Your world will be as one
Move forward as a whole
Do not divide each other
Only thoughts of love
All knowing will be yours
You will live as one

Mother Earth

Life is like Mother Earth; you keep spinning round in time.
Both slowly changing and adapting to different situations,
sustaining yourself, being nourished by food and air.

Listen to your own heartbeat, know your true self.
Listen to Mother Earth – she is reaching out to you; there is a
shift, she needs to heal, and you need to heal.

Find your inner light and light up the world.
Bring love and faith to the dark corners of life by speaking out;
let others hear your words.

One act of kindness brightens up Mother Earth.
One fewer act of non-pollution helps cleanse her; Mother Earth
sings her song; let her heal.

Guidance is the key to happiness from:

Your first breathe

Your first smile

Your first steps

Your first words

Your first actions

Your first love

Your first values

Live your talk

Walk your talk

Be true to yourself

Take this forward in your life
and teach others true love and guidance.

Carry our torch

Your heart is whole when linked with the soul.
Your mind is strong when calm and still.
Your energy vibrates when connected to us.
Your vibrations ripple out across the ethos.

We feel your heartbeat within our spirit.
We hear your mind's thoughts with ours.
We feel your vibration across our realm.
We touch your hand so you stay calm.

As we blend, our energies entwine.
Our love and light becomes your candle.
Our flame becomes your journey's path.
The candle will flicker but we will guide you.

You are our ambassadors, so carry our torch.
You take our messages across your time.
You will vibrate out our love into the world.
We are all one; be strong, trust and shine, my friends.

The future is yours

You make the path you follow.
You can all make this world as one.
You should help and support each other,
Not tear each other down.

Your thoughts make the future.
You need to radiate positive, loving thoughts.
You need to stand up and set the example.
You need to be strong and brave,
move forward and shine your light.

Your children are your future –
you need to listen to their innocent minds.
You need to let them change the world.
You need to show them the path of light,
let them shine; the future is theirs.

Your very essence is our essence,
your light is our light,
and we all shine as one.

Remember this while you walk
your life's path on Mother Earth, my friends.

Who's in the mirror?

Human, flesh and bone is how you see your reflection.
Your mirror reflects back what only your eyes see.
Mankind define themselves by what lies on top of the surface.

Step back from the mirror and look around you and beyond.
Now look beyond the horizon; do this with your fellow man,
too. You are truly defined by what lies beneath what you
cannot see.

You are all more than just a reflection, a glance in a mirror.
Look down deep within your own body; get to know yourself.
When you know what defines you, you can judge others in a
different way.

Now you see human, flesh, bone, spirit, pure essence and love.
Now your reflection in the mirror has expanded to the fill
the room.

Your soul now shines out from the mirror to reflect around
the world.

You are in the mirror, my friend.

Now, my friends please reflect on the words and messages in this book. They will all resonate differently with you, and help you move forward with your life's path, into the love and the light. If you feel doubt, that is your ego, but as you trust more and more, we will be around you; remember that what you feel is real, and your life will take on a whole new meaning. To find spiritualism you don't have to be a practitioner in healing, mediumship or holistic practices; you can find us through your spirit churches and centre's, or in your own choice of work and your home.

Find your spiritual path first and heal your own wounds, then the light will come in. If your path is then to be a light worker, you will be shown the way. Use your gift of intuition to know the answers to which path to take, and ask for signs and guidance; we will be there waiting for you, my friend.

We walk beside you every day my friends. Stay safe, live your life in the best way you can, in consideration of all others and you will shine; the divine is watching over you.

Love and blessings

Harold

I would like to thank my Utopian partners that have helped with this book. I would like to thank Sharon, my human friend on earth, for her patience and understanding of what we want to achieve in this book. I have found her heart is pure and we love her creative mind and imagination. Mind you, this writing is a challenge for her, as she is what you call dyslexic and struggles to write well and put her thoughts across on paper. With the help of a couple of her earth friends, we achieved a punctuated language you would understand and enjoy.

We have also created a lot of inspirational guidance messages with Sharon; we decided these would be cards, instead of a book. The set of cards are for daily guidance as individuals to use, or you can ask for guidance for family members or friends. Light workers will find them key in their day-to-day healing work for their clients too.

Sharon

I would first of all like to thank my awesome spirit team for their patience in working through me. I would like to thank all those people who have been a part of my life and those to come. I am thankful for all those lessons I have learned that have made me the person I am today. I am excited at the thought of what's to come, working with Spirit.

I would like to thank my family and friends who have travelled my light worker journey with me so far, for their support and understanding. Especially my husband, soul mate and best friend Chris; while others ridiculed me on my journey, he never questioned, only supported me in my beliefs.

https://twitter.com/SBengalrose
https://www.facebook.com/Bengalrosehealing
Sharon@bengalrose.co.uk
You can purchase the 'Inspiration Guidance Cards' from Bengalrose Healing www.bengalrose.co.uk

You are all as one
You live in divide
Come together as one
Be whole and true
Love and see as one
Be as one and shine

Live hand in hand
Walk side by side
Learn from each other
Teach each other
Support each other
Guide each other

Your world will be as one
Move forward as a whole
Do not divide each other
Only thoughts of love
All-knowing will be yours
You will live as one

We would all like to end this book with this AFFIRMATION for you to repeat on a daily basis x.

Grace hovers over me and helps me to see, as you would have me see. Be in my thinking and my understanding. In my speaking and my listening. In my heart and in my actions. That I may live my highest and best life right here, right now, as a channel of divine love.

Provided by my friend Karin from her spirit guide team x

Love and blessings to you all x

Made in the USA
Charleston, SC
14 December 2015